INTERNAL SORTING METHODS presents a well-written, logically organized, and thorough review of the alternative methods for sorting data files in the internal memory system of modern digital computers.

Sorting methods treated in this volume include integral methods, merging, ancestral sorting, counting, selection sorting, sorting in place, P-operator method, sifting (the Shell sort), partitioning (Quick-sort), and Treesort 3. Coverage also is devoted to file parameters, compile time procedures, and programming a standard sort as well as auxiliary procedures (random number generator and timing routines).

AMONG THE FEATURES

- Presents a very thorough discussion of useful internal sorting methods arranged in logical categories.

- Describes each method clearly and concisely, treats its advantages and disadvantages, and illustrates its use in a realistic example.

- Provides a working PL/1 program for each sorting method and includes timing results and storage requirements.

- Includes a complete and up-to-date bibliography that covers developments in both internal and external sorting.

- Provides concise descriptions of special data structures such as lists and trees.

A.B. degree from Hamilton College and the Ph.D. in Mathematics from the Johns Hopkins University. Dr. Rich is President of the Maryland Academy of Sciences.

INTERNAL SORTING

METHODS

Illustrated with PL/1 Programs

PRENTICE-HALL
SERIES IN AUTOMATIC COMPUTATION

George Forsythe, editor

AHO AND ULLMAN, *Theory of Parsing, Translation, and Compiling,*
    Volume I: Parsing

ANDREE, *Computer Programming: Techniques, Analysis, and Mathematics*

ANSELONE, *Collectively Compact Operator Approximation Theory*
    and Applications to Integral Equations

ARBIB, *Theories of Abstract Automata*

BATES AND DOUGLAS, *Programming Language/One,* 2nd ed.

BLUMENTHAL, *Management Information Systems*

BOBROW AND SCHWARTZ, *Computers and the Policy-Making Community*

BOWLES, editor, *Computers in Humanistic Research*

CESCHINO AND KUNTZMAN, *Numerical Solution of Initial Value Problems*

CRESS, et al., *FORTRAN IV with WATFOR and WATFIV*

DANIEL, *The Approximate Minimization of Functionals*

DESMONDE, *A Conversational Graphic Data Processing System*

DESMONDE, *Computers and Their Uses,* 2nd ed.

DESMONDE, *Real-Time Data Processing Systems*

EVANS, et al., *Simulation Using Digital Computers*

FIKE, *Computer Evaluation of Mathematical Functions*

FIKE, *PL/1 for Scientific Programmers*

FORSYTHE AND MOLER, *Computer Solution of Linear Algebraic Systems*

GAUTHIER AND PONTO, *Designing Systems Programs*

GEAR, *Numerical Initial Value Problems in Ordinary Differential Equations*

GOLDEN, *FORTRAN IV Programming and Computing*

GOLDEN AND LEICHUS, *IBM/360 Programming and Computing*

GORDON, *System Simulation*

GREENSPAN, *Lectures on the Numerical Solution of Linear, Singular and*
    Nonlinear Differential Equations

GRUENBERGER, editor, *Computers and Communications*

GRUENBERGER, editor, *Critical Factors in Data Management*

GRUENBERGER, editor, *Expanding Use of Computers in the 70's*

GRUENBERGER, editor, *Fourth Generation Computers*

HARTMANIS AND STEARNS, *Algebraic Structure Theory of Sequential Machines*

HULL, *Introduction to Computing*

JACOBY, et al., *Iterative Methods for Nonlinear Optimization Problems*

JOHNSON, *System Structure in Data, Programs, and Computers*

KANTER, *The Computer and the Executive*

KIVIAT, et al., *The SIMSCRIPT II Programming Language*

LORIN, *Parallelism in Hardware and Software: Real and Apparent Concurrency*

LOUDEN AND LEDIN, *Programming the IBM 1130,* 2nd ed.

MARTIN, *Design of Real-Time Computer Systems*

MARTIN, *Future Developments in Telecommunications*

MARTIN, *Man-Computer Dialogue*

MARTIN, *Programming Real-Time Computing Systems*

MARTIN, *Systems Analysis for Data Transmission*

MARTIN, *Telecommunications and the Computer*

MARTIN, *Teleprocessing Network Organization*

MARTIN AND NORMAN, *The Computerized Society*

MATHISON AND WALKER, *Computers and Telecommunications: Issues in Public Policy*

MCKEEMAN, et al., *A Compiler Generator*

MINSKY, *Computation: Finite and Infinite Machines*

MOORE, *Interval Analysis*

PLANE AND MCMILLAN, *Discrete Optimization: Integer Programming and Network Analysis for Management Decisions*

PRITSKER AND KIVIAT, *Simulation with GASP II: a FORTRAN-Based Simulation Language*

PYLYSHYN, editor, *Perspectives on the Computer Revolution*

RICH, *Internal Sorting Methods Illustrated with PL/1 Programs*

RUSTIN, editor, *Computer Networks*

RUSTIN, editor, *Debugging Techniques in Large Systems*

RUSTIN, editor, *Formal Semantics of Programming Languages*

SACKMAN AND CITRENBAUM, editors, *On-Line Planning: Towards Creative Problem-Solving*

SALTON, editor, *The SMART Retrieval System: Experiments in Automatic Document Processing*

SAMMET, *Programming Languages: History and Fundamentals*

SCHULTZ, *Digital Processing: A System Orientation*

SCHULTZ, *Finite Element Analysis*

SCHWARZ, et al., *Numerical Analysis of Symmetric Matrices*

SHERMAN, *Techniques in Computer Programming*

SIMON AND SIKLOSSY, editors, *Representation and Meaning: Experiments with Information Processing Systems*

SNYDER, *Chebyshev Methods in Numerical Approximation*

STERLING AND POLLACK, *Introduction to Statistical Data Processing*

STOUTMEYER, *PL/1 Programming for Engineering and Science*

STROUD, *Approximate Calculation of Multiple Integrals*

STROUD AND SECREST, *Gaussian Quadrature Formulas*

TAVISS, editor, *The Computer Impact*

TRAUB, *Iterative Methods for the Solution of Polynomial Equations*

VAN TASSEL, *Computer Security Management*

VARGA, *Matrix Iterative Analysis*

VAZSONYI, *Problem Solving by Digital Computers with PL/1 Programming*

WAITE, *Implementing Software for Non-Numeric Application*

WILKINSON, *Rounding Errors in Algebraic Processes*

ZIEGLER, *Time-Sharing Data Processing Systems*

PRENTICE-HALL INTERNATIONAL, INC., *London*
PRENTICE-HALL OF AUSTRALIA, PTY. LTD., *Sydney*
PRENTICE-HALL OF CANADA, LTD., *Toronto*
PRENTICE-HALL OF INDIA PRIVATE LIMITED, *New Delhi*
PRENTICE-HALL OF JAPAN, INC., *Tokyo*

INTERNAL SORTING
METHODS
Illustrated with PL/1 Programs

ROBERT P. RICH

Applied Physics Laboratory
The Johns Hopkins University

PRENTICE-HALL, INC.

ENGLEWOOD CLIFFS, NEW JERSEY

Library of Congress Cataloging in Publication Data

RICH, ROBERT P.
   Internal sorting methods illustrated with PL/1
programs.

   Bibliography: p.
   1. Sorting (Electronic computers)   2. PL/1
(Computer program language)   I. Title.
QA76.5.R473   001.6'442   71–39111
ISBN   0–13–472357–0

Current printing (last digit):

10   9   8   7   6   5   4   3   2   1

Printed in the United States of America

CONTENTS

CONTENTS

CONTENTS

PREFACE

Sorting items, or arranging them in order according to a portion of each item called its key, presents an interesting and useful application for a digital computer. If the number of items is so great that not all of them will fit at once into the main memory of the computer, then it is a question of external sorting using magnetic tapes, disks or other peripheral units. We deal here rather with internal sorting of files or parts of files which can be held in the main memory.

Each major internal sorting method is discussed and illustrated by a PL/1 program, with space and timing information given. The resulting set of programming examples should be of interest even to those whose interest in sorting is secondary.

The bibliography is as complete as possible and covers external as well as internal sorting.

It is a pleasure to acknowledge the assistance of Mrs. Betty E. Hess in the computer editing of the text and Mrs. Wilda B. Newman in the tracing of bibliographic items.

INTERNAL SORTING

METHODS

Illustrated with PL/1 Programs

1. Introduction.

Much of the early work on computer sorting was done for machines with small internal memories, operated in a one-job-at-a-time mode. Most of the time during a typical run was spent reading and writing peripherals: tapes or disks.

The advent of larger internal memories and the time-shared mode of operation has increased the relative importance of internal sorting because: 1) with large internal memory fewer applications require an external sort; 2) even if external sorting is required, the internal sorting of large segments can take a substantial amount of time; 3) the number of peripheral passes is reduced by preliminary internal sorting of large segments; 4) running several jobs at once means that time spent waiting for peripherals need not be wasted.

It seemed useful, therefore, to survey the available methods for internal sorting, especially for large files, in order to choose a method suitable for general use. The bibliography developed during this survey (par. 84) includes references for external as well as internal sorting, since many papers deal with both and a similar survey for external methods should be made when opportunity offers.

The survey disclosed an astonishing variety of methods and indicated the value of this topic for teaching of computer science and training in practical programming.

This value rests on several characteristics of sorting procedures. For one thing, internal sort routines run from about a dozen statements (e.g., successive minima, par. 44) to more than a gross (e.g., natural merging, par. 24), comfortably covering the span of complexity appropriate for examples and exercises. The logical complexity covers a comparable range.

A variety of data structures occur in the routines in a natural way, and extensions to more sophisticated structures are easily motivated and exemplified.

Consequently, the several algorithms provide a reasonable test of language features. An attempt to sort an alphabetic list in Fortran, Algol or Basic, for example, or to translate Quicksort (par. 62) into Cobol is enlightening.

The question of why the chain merge (par. 27) writes itself easily without GOTO's while the straight merge (par. 25) does not illustrates the helpfulness of this topic in a discussion of programming techniques.

It is therefore not surprising that early proofs of correctness (London 1970, Hoare 1971) were in this and related areas.

The fact that the function of a sort program is so easy to specify, of course, not only helps in a formal proof of correctness but also facilitates checkout in the usual sense: feed the routine a set of random files and verify that each is sorted correctly.

Internal Sorting
1. Introduction.

The wide range of data structures and techniques that permits a useful comparison of languages also permits the selection of a representative set of benchmarks for comparison of computers, compilers, and operating systems.

Although some of the methods have been subjected to mathematical analysis, there are still many questions for which experimental answers are indicated (e.g., the optimal storage ratio, par. 16). Systematic instruction in the use of the computer as an experimental laboratory deserves more attention than it receives in many curricula.

In order to provide a useful comparison, each method was programmed in PL/1 and run on a consistent sample of files to obtain comparable numbers for program size and sorting time. The program and detailed results are given under each method tested, and a summary table is provided in par. 66.

Programs for some of the methods (e.g., the Patience sort (par. 48)) have not previously been published, and improvements in the published algorithms (e.g., Quicksort, par. 62) are suggested.

While it is true that the timing comparisons depend on the particular conditions (par. 8) used for the tests as well as the computer and language used, a consistent series of results of this form still has a certain value in narrowing the choices among the many methods available.

The survey and accompanying experimentation indicate that Hoare's Quicksort (par. 62), with a special mechanism for equal items, provides a good compromise among the various boundary conditions.

A number of general topics dealing with sorting are discussed in par. 2.

2. Preliminary Considerations.

Before we discuss specific sorting methods, it is convenient to consider a number of points, both notational and conceptual.

3. Keyed Files.

A _file_ X(1:n) is a sequence X(1),X(2),...,X(n) of _items_ X(i). A _segment_ X(a:b) of the file is a subsequence X(a), X(a+1),...,X(b-1),X(b) of consecutive items. The _length_ of a segment X(a:b) is the number b-a+1 of items in it, with the convention that if b<a then the length of the segment is zero. Thus, for example, the whole file X(1:n) is a segment of length n.

A file is said to be _keyed_ when a mapping K of items to real numbers has been defined, so that for each i ($1 \leq i \leq n$), KX(i) is a uniquely defined real number. Each such key mapping defines a linear order relation on the items of the file, called the sorting order or collating sequence. Thus, X(i) precedes X(j) in the sort order if and only if $KX(i) \leq KX(j)$.

We say that the file is _in sort_ if i<j implies that $KX(i) \leq KX(j)$.

Internal Sorting
2. Preliminary Considerations.
   3. Keyed Files.

The key mapping may be a simple one, as in the case where the items $X(i)$ are numbers and $KX(i) = X(i)$, yielding a numerical sort in ascending order, or $KX(i) = -X(i)$, yielding a numerical sort in descending order.

But since the file items may be data structures of any complexity, since the sort may involve several data fields within each item, and since the ordering rules for each field may be complicated (e.g., the ordering of names in an index), the specification of the mapping function K may be very complex in particular cases, and its implementation on the computer may be quite time-consuming.

Unless the sorting method specifically requires the key, as integral methods (par. 12) do, the key need not actually be converted to numerical form; all that is necessary is that it be possible to compare items correctly.

In most applications each item contains not only the key $KX(i)$ but also some additional data $DX(i)$. A unit of data within an item is called a _field_. A particular field may be part of $KX(i)$ during one operation on the file and part of $DX(i)$ during another operation on the file.

An example may help to clarify the discussion at this point. Consider a personnel file for a hypothetical organization, with the following fields in each item.

1) employee number (four digits);
2) organizational code (three characters, specifying division, group and project);
3) supervisory code (one character);
4) year of birth;
5) year hired;
6) occupational specialty (four characters);
7) monthly salary;
8) building number;
9) room number;
10) telephone extension;
11) name;

A file item might look like this, with fields separated by semicolons:

1234;CFA;2;1925;1952;PR23;615.23;12;313;7942;Doe, John D.

The protocol file is kept in order by employee number, field 1, and all changes to the file are sorted on this field before being applied to the protocol in an update.

The directory is obtained by extracting fields 11, 8, 9, 10, and 2 and then sorting alphabetically by name.

The organizational table is obtained by extracting fields 2, 3, 6, and 11 and sorting with the organizational code as major key and the name as minor key.

The pension committee is interested in a special listing

obtained by extracting fields 4, 6, 7, 11 and sorting on all four fields, in that order of decreasing significance.

4. Sorting.

The process of rearranging a file X(1:n) so that it is in sort with respect to a key mapping K is called sorting the file. Different sorting algorithms may be compared from several different points of view: computing speed, program complexity, storage and peripheral resources required, and so on.
Let us look at some of these considerations.

5. Random Access.

Some sorting methods require that all items of the file be accessible to the computer before the process is begun, and some (e.g., ranking sort (par. 45)) treat the items of the file one at a time in their original sequence, so that later items are not considered (and hence need not be accessible to the computer) until earlier ones have been taken care of.
On the other hand, some sorting methods (e.g., minima sort (par. 44)), having dealt with an item, do not need to refer to it again, so that it need not remain accessible to the computer thereafter, while other methods do not finish with an item until the sort is complete.
Some methods (e.g., transposition (par. 38)) require several passes over the file, and are such that only a few adjacent items need be accessible at any one time for each pass.
We are interested here in internal sorting, in which the whole file (or that consecutive portion of it currently to be sorted) is in the internal memory of the computer, so that all items are equally accessible during the sorting process.

6. Extra Storage.

Internal sorting methods may be distinguished by the amount of storage required to sort a file of length n.
This storage must include the sorting program itself, but this requirement is usually ignored in general treatments, since it is typically a small fraction of the total storage (for large files, at least).
Storage must also be allocated to the file itself, at least one copy of which must be held in internal memory during the sorting process (by definition, for an internal sort).
Some sorting methods require that additional storage be assigned for additional copies of the file or for pointers to locations of file items. The number of such pointers needed may be proportional to n, to log n, etc.
Other things being equal, we will prefer a method for which the amount of this additional storage is as small as possible.

Internal Sorting
2. Preliminary Considerations.
    4. Sorting.
        7. Sequence Preservation.

7. Sequence Preservation.

For a particular mapping function K we may perfectly well have $KX(i) = KX(j)$ even when $X(i)$ and $X(j)$ are not exactly the same. Also, a particular file may have pairs of identical items in it.

For some purposes we are interested in whether or not the sorting method is sequence-preserving, that is, in whether or not items with equal keys preserve their original order during the sort.

8. Sorting Time.

The time $T(n)$ required for an internal sort of a file of n items depends on a large number of factors, including:

1. the sorting method used,
2. the efficiency with which the method is programmed, including the effect of a higher level language if one is used,
3. the characteristics of the computer,
4. the original order of the file,
5. the complexity of the key mapping function,
6. the length and/or structural complexity of the file items.

In this survey we are primarily interested in the effect of the sorting method on the sorting time, and less interested in the effects of the other factors mentioned above.

In most of the experimentation, therefore, we keep these other factors as constant as possible by using one language (PL/1) on one computer (IBM 360/91 under OS/MVT) with one degree of programming skill (the author's). The file items are halfword integers with random initial order and the identity key mapping: $KX(i) = X(i)$. The effects of departure from this standard case will be discussed as appropriate.

A number of the more interesting methods were programmed as procedures. A control program was written to generate a random file, call the sort procedure, and repeat, to get a sample of sorting times for fixed n; the sample size was usually 40. The whole process was then carried out for other values of n to permit an estimate of the timing function $T(n)$.

The storage required for each of the procedures was estimated from the compiler printout by adding all the storage for the whole program (including driver) and then subtracting 21094 bytes for the driver.

Internal Sorting
2. Preliminary Considerations.
    4. Sorting.
        8. Sorting Time.

The timing was done by reference to the system clock via the STIMER and TTIMER routines (par. 82). The least count of this clock is 104 microseconds, so that the times for small values of n are subject to quantizing error. Also, the time returned by TTIMER depends, in the timeshared environment, on the other jobs currently in the system; hence, even for larger values of n, the timing results are not reproducible to better than about 7%.

If T(n) is approximately proportional to some function f(n) for sufficiently large n then we say that T(n) is of order f(n). For example, we shall see that some sorting methods are of order n², some are of order n log n, and so on.

---

9. Sorting by Surrogate.

A surrogate for a file X(1:n) is a data structure S by means of which each item of X is uniquely identified.

The most obvious surrogate is a location vector L(1:n) each of whose items is the subscript i of an item X(i). But other surrogate structures such as lists and trees may also be used.

If the computation of the key KX(i) of an item X(i) is a time-consuming operation, then it may be wise to do this computation only once for each item and store the result in the surrogate, so that the surrogate for X(i) would be an ordered pair (KX(i),i). If the sorting method used is not sequence preserving then using the original subscript i as an additional (least significant) subkey will ensure sequence preservation.

The actual sorting operations are then carried out on the surrogates, with reference to the original items as necessary if the key is not part of the surrogate. The locations of the original items are left unchanged during this step.

When the surrogates are in sort order, the original items are then put in the same order. This usually requires additional storage for a second copy of the file. But if, for instance, this is part of an external sort then the items may be written to output in surrogate order, and a second internal copy of the file is not required.

The use of surrogates is helpful when the original items are long (so that their movement from place to place is time-consuming), or of variable length (so that the interchange of two items is cumbersome), or, as mentioned above, when the key calculation is complicated.

Any of the methods described below may be carried out by surrogate, and this possibility will not usually be mentioned for each method. A few methods actually require surrogates of one sort or another.

10. Vector Trees.

For any integers m>1 and h>0 we define a complete (m,h)-tree as a set of nodes, each node being on one of h levels. There is a single node, called the root, on the first (lowest) level. If j<h then each node on the j-th level has precisely m filial nodes; nodes on the h-th (highest) level have no filial nodes and are called terminal nodes. If 1<j≤h then each node on the j-th level has precisely one paternal node, and is one of the filial nodes of this paternal node.

A convenient way of implementing a complete (m,h)-tree is by means of a vector V(1:k), where

$$k = (m**h-1)/(m-1).$$

We let V(1) be the root of the tree. For any j < k/m, the filial nodes of the node V(j) are the m consecutive components

$$V(mj-m+2),...,V(mj+1).$$

Thus, for example, if m=2, then the root V(1) has the two sons V(2), V(3). V(2) has the sons V(4), V(5); V(3) has the sons V(6), V(7); and so on.

If m=3 then the root V(1) has the three sons V(2), V(3), V(4). V(2) has the sons V(5), V(6), V(7). V(3) has the sons V(8), V(9), V(10); and so on.

If the multiplicity m=2, then we have a binary tree. Complete binary vector trees are used in the tournament sort (par. 35) and in Treesort 3 (par. 65). The generalization to m>2 is useful in the discussion of selection sorting (par. 33).

Usually a vector tree is used as a surrogate for the file X(1:n), so that each node points to a file item, or is zero to indicate that it does not point to a file item. That is, V(j) points to the item X(V(j)) if V(j)>0. But in other applications V(j) may actually contain a file item rather than pointing to it.

The first use of this vector numbering of the nodes of binary trees was apparently (Isenburg 1940 page 8) used by Michael Eizinger in 1590 for genealogical tables; the method was revived by Stephan Kekule von Stradonitz in 1898, and is now in general use for ancestral tables.

11. Sorting Methods.

We are now ready to survey the various sorting methods that have been proposed, so that an appropriate selection can be made to meet particular needs.

Illustrative examples will be given at various points in the text. Each example will usually start with a file of integers to be put in ascending numerical order. We shall frequently enclose a segment of this file in parentheses to indicate that it is not

Internal Sorting
11. Sorting Methods.

yet sorted, or in square brackets to indicate that it is in sort.
Thus we might start with the unsorted file

(4 2 7 5 8 1 3 9 6)

and indicate those segments which are already in sort as follows

([4][2 7][5 8][1 3 9][6]).

If we merged (par. 23) adjacent pairs of strings we would get

([2 4 7][1 3 5 8 9][6]).

Merging again would give

([1 2 3 4 5 7 8 9][6]),

and a final merge would give the sorted file

[1 2 3 4 5 6 7 8 9].

12. Integral Methods.

We look first at methods requiring that the key mapping be
into positive integers, so that KX(i) is a positive integer for
each i. While it is true that any key mapping can be transformed
into an integral mapping, the methods described in this section
are of practical interest only if the range of the keys is not
too large.

13. Address Sorting.

In address sorting, each file item is put into a location
determined from its key by a simple address calculation. Given
the file

(4 2 7 5 8 1 3 9 6)

of nine items, we might provide 15 such locations, as indicated
by the dots in the array

    . . . .

Putting each item x in turn into the location [1.5x] gives
the sequence

Internal Sorting
11. Sorting Methods.
    12. Integral Methods.
        13. Address Sorting.

```
.  .  .  .  .  4  .  .  .  .  .  .  .  .  .
.  2  .  .  .  4  .  .  .  .  .  .  .  .  .
.  2  .  .  .  4  .  .  7  .  .  .  .  .  .
.  2  .  .  .  4  5  .  .  7  .  .  .  .  .
.  2  .  .  .  4  5  .  .  7  .  8  .  .  .
1  2  .  .  .  4  5  .  .  7  .  8  .  .  .
1  2  .  3  .  4  5  .  .  7  .  8  .  .  .
1  2  .  3  .  4  5  .  .  7  .  8  9  .  .
1  2  .  3  .  4  5  .  6  7  .  8  9  .  .
```

If we now copy the items back into their original places, ignoring the unused locations, we get the sorted file

[1 2 3 4 5 6 7 8 9].

Let us now state the process more formally, and consider some of the complications that arise.

Let $F(i) = f(KX(i))$ be a mapping of the keys $KX(i)$ of a file $X(1:n)$ to positive integers. Such a mapping is called order preserving if

$KX(i) \le KX(j)$ implies $F(i) \le F(j)$.

The mapping is called proper if the minimum possible value of $F(i)$, for any legal key, is 1, and the maximum possible value of $F(i)$, for any legal key, is some number $M > n$. The ratio $r = M/n$ is then called the storage ratio of the mapping f.

A proper order preserving function f is called an address mapping function, and may be used in a sort method called "address calculation sorting" in the following way.

Let $Z(1:M)$ be a work area capable of holding file items. Before the sort begins, mark each location $Z(j)$ as "empty" by some suitable convention.

For each file item $X(i)$ in turn, look at the location $Z(F(i))$. If this location is still empty then put $X(i)$ in it. But if this location already contains a file item, then invoke an adjustment algorithm to put $X(i)$ into a nearby empty location $Z(j)$. The adjustment algorithm is said to be ordered if all the items in Z at any time are in sort, disordered if they are not.

When all file items have been moved to Z, they are then copied back to X; the empty locations that still exist in Z (since the storage ratio is assumed to be greater than 1) are of course skipped over.

If an ordered adjustment algorithm was used, the sort is now complete.

Internal Sorting
11. Sorting Methods.
    12. Integral Methods.
        13. Address Sorting.

If a disordered adjustment algorithm was used, then the local departures from correct sort order must be corrected, either while the items are being copied from Z to X or in a separate pass over X when the copying has been completed, using a sorting method (e.g., ranking sort (par. 45)) that takes advantage of the ordering that then already exists.

This method appears to be due to Isaac and Singleton (1956). Under ideal conditions it is of timing order n, the smallest order for any method known. Proper use of the method requires the choice of mapping function (par. 14), adjustment algorithm (par. 15) and storage ratio (par. 16).

14. Choice of Mapping Function.

The method works best when the images $F(i) = f(KX(i))$ are evenly spread on the interval $(1,M)$. In the limiting case in which the file is a permutation of the first M positive integers, each item can be put immediately into its proper place in Z, and no adjustment or compacting is necessary.

The next simplest case is the one used as an example in the present document: the keys $KX(i)$ have a rectangular random distribution on the interval (A,B). In this case the simple linear mapping

$$F(i) = M(KX(i)-A)/(B-A) + 1$$

may be used, so that the images $F(i)$ have a rectangular distribution on the interval $(1,M)$.

If the keys $KX(i)$ are numbers, but the cumulative distribution function is not a straight line, then this distribution function may be approximated by a sequence of straight line segments (a frequency polygon) to get the mapping function f. This technique is discussed in detail by Kronmal and Tarter (1965).

If the distribution function is not known in advance, it may be estimated by means of a sample drawn from the file before the actual sort begins.

If the keys are not intrinsically numeric (e.g., as in sorting by names) then a preliminary conversion to numbers will be required.

The fact that address sorting is not more widely used, in spite of its high speed, is due mainly to the problem of determining a suitable mapping f; the problem is intensified when it is a question of designing a general purpose routine. Of course the relatively large amount of additional storage required is also a factor in the decision.

Internal Sorting
11. Sorting Methods.
    12. Integral Methods.
        13. Address Sorting.
            15. Adjustment Algorithms.

15. Adjustment Algorithms.

When the location $Z(F(i))$ into which we would like to put the item $X(i)$ is already full, it is necessary to invoke an adjustment algorithm to find a nearby location $Z(j)$ which can be used instead.

Isaac and Singleton used an ordered adjustment algorithm, shifting the positions of nearby items in Z so that the new item is inserted in the proper sort order. The details are given in Flores (1969 chapter 6).

An alternative approach is to take the "nearest" empty location, and to make the necessary local corrections of sort order later, after all items have been copied into Z. If we take the word "nearest" in its literal sense, then we scan in both directions from $Z(F(i))$ to find an empty location $Z(j)$, so that j is sometimes greater than $F(i)$ and sometimes less. This approach requires a slightly more complicated program and results in a method which is not sequence-preserving.

It is probably better, therefore, to take the nearest following empty location, scanning only toward the end of Z, so that j is always greater than $F(i)$. If this is done, then a few extra locations should be provided at the end of Z to take care of overflows. The program must also provide for a forward block shift of the tail end of Z in case not enough extra positions have been provided.

The number of extra positions needed (so that the block shift is only rarely needed) depends on the file size and storage ratio in quite a complicated way.

16. Storage Ratio.

The ratio $r = M/n$ of the amount of additional storage to the file size must clearly be greater than or equal to unity or the method will not work at all.

As r increases, the number of adjustments decreases, and the sorting time tends to decrease. On the other hand, as r increases, the number of empty locations in Z that must be ignored (and hence tested for empty) during compaction increases, and the total time for the sort therefore tends to increase. The net result of these two factors is that sorting time (for fixed n, as r increases) first decreases and then increases, yielding a single minimum for some value r=R. The curve is quite flat in the neighborhood of the minimum (as we would expect) and the choice of R is not very critical from the practical point of view.

Internal Sorting
11. Sorting Methods.
     12. Integral Methods.
          13. Address Sorting.
               16. Storage Ratio.

The minimizing value R depends on the details of the sort. Isaac and Singleton found an experimental value R=2.4. Flores (1960) derives formulas for the number of operations involved and suggests the value R=2. These results are both for an ordered adjustment algorithm.

For the disordered adjustment algorithm used in the procedure below, a run was made with file size n=1073 and various values of the storage ratio r. A sample of 40 sorts was done for each value of r to get the mean sorting time T in milliseconds, with the following results.

r= 1.60 1.70 1.80 1.90 2.00 2.10 2.20 2.30 2.40 2.50 2.60 2.70
T= 4.71 4.61 4.59 4.59 4.63 4.60 4.64 4.71 4.75 4.81 4.85 4.94

It appears that for this procedure the minimum falls at about r = 1.8, with not much difference in the range from 1.6 to 2.3. One would tend to prefer the smaller end of the range to economize on storage.

It is not surprizing that the optimum ratio is smaller for the disordered approach, since the ordered algorithm exacts a greater penalty for each adjustment.

17. The Procedure.

The procedure shown below uses a disordered adjustment algorithm, taking always the first empty location at or above the one indicated by the mapping function. The timing results are given for a storage ratio

$$r = (2n+20)/n,$$

which is larger than the optimum determined in par. 16.
The procedure is sequence-preserving as shown.

```
SRT:  PROC(N); /* ADDRESS SORT */
      DCL N FIXED BIN(15);  /* FILE SIZE */
      DCL Z(30000) FIXED BIN(15); /* SORTING SPACE */
      DCL K FIXED BIN(31);  /* ADDRESS */
      DCL KM FIXED BIN(31); /* CONVERSION FACTOR */
      DCL KN FLOAT BIN INIT(2);
      DCL XM FIXED BIN(15) INIT(10000); /* MAXIMUM KEY */
      DCL (I,J,JN,L) FIXED BIN(15);
      KM = KN*N;              /* CONVERSION FACTOR */
      JN = KM + 20;           /* SPACE ACTUALLY USED */
      DO I = 1 TO JN;         /* MARK Z AS EMPTY */
         Z(I) = -1;
         END;
      DO I = 1 TO N;          /* STORE EACH ITEM */
         K = 1 + KM*X(I)/XM;
```

Internal Sorting
11. Sorting Methods.
    12. Integral Methods.
        13. Address Sorting.
            17. The Procedure.

```
            DO J = K TO JN;
               IF Z(J)=-1 THEN DO;
                  Z(J) = X(I);
                  GO TO SRTD;
                  END;
               END;
            DO J = 1 TO JN; /* IF NO EMPTY, SHIFT DOWN */
               IF Z(J)=-1 THEN DO;
                  DO L = J TO JN-1;
                     Z(L) = Z(L+1);
                     END;
                  Z(JN) = X(I);
                  GO TO SRTD;
                  END;
               END;
  SRTD:    END;
          /* ALL ITEMS ARE NOW IN Z. COPY BACK TO X. */
          I = 0;                    /* POINTER TO X */
          DO J = 1 TO JN;
             IF Z(J)=-1 THEN;
             ELSE DO;
                DO L = I BY -1 TO 1 WHILE(Z(J)<X(L));
                   X(L+1) = X(L);
                   END;
                X(L+1) = Z(J);
                I = I + 1;
                END;
             END;
          RETURN;
          END SRT;
```

The timing results are as follows, where

```
N = file size
T = sorting time in milliseconds
A = 100T/(N LOG2(N))
B = 100T/N
C = number of comparisons
R = number of replacements.
```
A superscript means multiplication by that power of 10.

N=	1	2	4	7	11	18	29	46	72	114
T=	.799	.822	.820	.869	1.21	1.48	1.87	2.66	3.75	5.46
A=	79.9	41.1	10.2	4.42	3.19	1.97	1.33	1.05	.843	.701
B=	79.9	41.1	21.0	12.4	11.0	8.22	6.46	5.78	5.21	4.79
C=	24.0	28.5	36.9	50.9	71.2	106.	156.	235.	361.	561.
R=	24.0	28.1	36.3	48.9	66.6	97.2	144.	216.	328.	507.

Internal Sorting
11. Sorting Methods.
　12. Integral Methods.
　　13. Address Sorting.
　　　17. The Procedure.

N=	179	280	439	686	1073	1677	2621	4096	6400	10000
T=	8.27	12.8	19.0	29.3	45.2	70.8	111.	170.	267.	415.
A=	.617	.562	.494	.453	.419	.394	.374	.347	.330	.313
B=	4.62	4.57	4.33	4.27	4.21	4.22	4.24	4.17	4.18	4.15
C=	871.	1367	2118	3296	5149	8008	1245^1	1947^1	3054^1	4818^1
R=	787.	1226	1903	2958	4612	7172	1114^1	1729^1	2683^1	4139^1

The quantity　B　in the table is included to verify that the procedure is in fact of timing order n.

The storage required is 1034 bytes plus 2rn for the additional storage.

_____

18. Pigeon Hole Sort.
_____

The pigeonhole sort is a modification of address sorting.

M bins are provided for intermediate storage of the items, and a number Q is chosen so that MQ is greater than or equal to the file size n. The item X(i) is put into the [X(i)/Q]th bin. The items in each bin are then sorted.

Given the file

(4 2 7 5 8 1 3 9 6),

for example, we might take M=4, Q=3, and fill the four bins as follows:

(2 1) (4 5 3) (7 8 6) (9).

We sort each bin separately to get

[1 2][3 4 5][6 7 8][9]

and the file is in sort.

The version shown below rearranges the items in place, and uses a global ranking sort for the final adjustment. Inspection of the program will show that time could be saved if a second copy of the file were used to hold the bins. If the average bin is large, then a Shell sort within bins would be faster than global ranking.

This method requires (as written) a pointer vector P(0:M) and a bit vector B(1:n) to keep track of which items are not yet in the proper place.

The method is not sequence-preserving as written, and it is not clear how this defect can easily be overcome.

The procedure is as follows.

```
SRT:    PROC(N); /* PIGEON HOLE SORT */
        DCL (N,I,J,P(0:1000),M,Y,Q) FIXED BIN(15);
        DCL B(10000) BIT(1);
```

Internal Sorting
11. Sorting Methods.
    12. Integral Methods.
        18. Pigeon Hole Sort.


```
    M = N/10 + 1;            /* FIND MODULUS */
    Q = 10000/M;
    M = 10000/Q;
    DO WHILE (M>1000);
      Q = Q + 1;
      M = 10000/Q;
      END;
    DO I = 0 TO M;           /* INITIALIZE */
      P(I) = 0;
      END;
    DO I = 1 TO N;           /* FIND SIZE OF BINS */
      B(I) = '1'B;
      J = X(I)/Q + 1;
      P(J) = P(J) + 1;
      END;
    P(0) = 1;                /* SET BIN POINTERS */
    DO I = 1 TO M-1;
      P(I) = P(I) + P(I-1);
      END;
    DO I = 1 TO N;           /* PUT ITEMS IN BINS */
      DO WHILE (B(I));
        J = X(I)/Q;
        IF I = P(J) THEN DO;
          B(I) = '0'B;
          P(J) = P(J) + 1;
          END;
        ELSE DO;
          Y = X(P(J));
          X(P(J)) = X(I);
          X(I) = Y;
          B(P(J)) = '0'B;
          P(J) = P(J) + 1;
          END;
        END;
      END;
    DO J = 1 TO N-1;         /* FINAL RANKING SORT */
      Y = X(J+1);
      DO I = J BY -1 TO 1 WHILE (Y<X(I));
        X(I+1) = X(I);
        END;
      X(I+1) = Y;
      END;
    RETURN;
    END SRT;
```

The timing results are as follows, where

N = file size
T = sorting time in milliseconds
A = 100T/(N LOG2(N))

Internal Sorting
11. Sorting Methods.
    12. Integral Methods.
        18. Pigeon Hole Sort.

N=	1	2	4	7	11	18	29	46	72	114
T=	.539	.687	.908	1.30	1.86	2.83	4.37	6.73	10.3	16.4
A=	53.9	34.4	11.3	6.62	4.89	3.78	3.10	2.65	2.31	2.11

N=	179	280	439	686	1073	1677	2621	4096	6400	10000
T=	25.3	41.1	64.6	134.	243.	343.	419.	905.	1388	1379
A=	1.89	1.81	1.68	2.08	2.25	1.91	1.41	1.84	1.72	1.04

The storage required is 1418 bytes plus n/8 bytes for the binary vector B plus 2002 bytes for the vector P.

In the procedure above the modulus M was taken as one-tenth of the file size, simply to show a specific example. Increasing M increases the additional storage required and, by reducing the average number of items per bin, reduces the time required for the final sort within bins. The amount of time saved depends on the method used for this final sort, and is counterbalanced (for large M) by the number of empty bins that must be passed over.

The distribution of the number of items per bin is roughly Poisson for a random file, and of course the larger bins will dominate the time required for the final sort.

The choice of optimum modulus clearly needs further investigation.

An interesting variant of the pigeon hole sort is described in Outrata (1966).

----
19. Upward Radix Sort.

We illustrate the upward radix sort by a preliminary example using a binary radix.

Given the original file

(4 2 7 5 8 1 3 9 6)

we first convert each item to binary to get the equivalent file

(0100 0010 0111 0101 1000 0001 0011 1001 0110).

We now separate the items into two bins, according as the last digit is 0 or 1, leaving the relative order unchanged within each bin:

(0100 0010 1000 0110) (0111 0101 0001 0011 1001).

We divide the resulting string into two bins, using the next-to-last digit in the same way:

(0100 1000 0101 0001 1001) (0010 0110 0111 0011).

Repeat the same operation using the second digit:

Internal Sorting
11. Sorting Methods.
    12. Integral Methods.
        19. Upward Radix Sort.

(1000 0001 1001 0010 0011) (0100 0101 0110 0111).

Repeat again, using the first digit:

(0001 0010 0011 0100 0101 0110 0111)(1000 1001).

Conversion back to decimal shows that the file is now in order.
    A more formal and generalized statement of the method will
now be easy to follow.
    Let K be an integral key mapping function whose maximum
value is M. Let r(1),r(2),...,r(k) be a set of integers, each
greater than 1, whose product is greater than or equal to M. The
number r(j) is called the j-th (ascending) <u>radix</u>.
    Assign storage for r(1) "bins", each bin containing locati-
ons in which file items can be put. Number these bins 0,1,...,
r(1)-1. Each bin is originally empty. Now for each item X(1),
X(2),... in turn compute b(i) = MOD(KX(i),r(1)) and K(1)X(i) =
[KX(i)/r(1)]. Put the item X(i) in the next available location of
the b(i)-th bin.
    When all items of the original file have been put into bins,
form a single file consisting of the contents of bin 0 followed
by the contents of bin 1, and so on, with the contents of bin
r(1)-1 at the end.
    Now repeat the process on this new file, using r(2) bins and
the mapping function K(1).
    And so continue, until the process has been completed for
the last radix r(k).
    The resulting file will be in sort by original key K.
    This is a generalization of the process used on the punched
card sorter. It is sometimes called a column sort.
    The implementation of the "bins" is usually by list proces-
sing techniques, so that, typically, about 2n additional storage
locations are required.
    The number of item-handlings is kn, where each item-handling
is the work of modular arithmetic and bin assignment.
    The case where each radix r(j)=2 is called an upward binary
radix sort. If the keys KX(i) are dense on the interval (1,M)
then k is approximately LOG2(n), and the sorting time is then
proportional to n LOG2(n).
    This radix sort is called "upward" since the least signifi-
cant digit (to the base r(1)) is treated first and the most
significant digit (to the base r(k)) last, so the radices
increase in significance during the process.
    A procedure for an upward binary radix sort is given below.
It is sequence-preserving in the form given.

```
SRT:   PROC(N); /* ASCENDING BINARY RADIX SORT */
       DCL (I,J,I0,I1,N,M,Y0(10000),Y1(10000)) FIXED BIN(15);
       DCL B BIT(16) DEF M;
```

Internal Sorting
11. Sorting Methods.
    12. Integral Methods.
        19. Upward Radix Sort.


```
        DO J = 16 BY -1 TO 2; /* DO EACH BIT POSITION */
          I0 = 0;
          I1 = 0;
          DO I = 1 TO N;          /* SPLIT THE FILE */
            M = X(I);
            IF SUBSTR(B,J,1) THEN DO;
              I1 = I1 + 1;
              Y1(I1) = X(I);
              END;
            ELSE DO;
              I0 = I0 + 1;
              Y0(I0) = X(I);
              END;
            END;
          DO I = 1 TO I0;         /* REJOIN THE FILE */
            X(I) = Y0(I);
            END;
          DO I = 1 TO I1;
            X(I+I0) = Y1(I);
            END;
          END;
        RETURN;
        END SRT;
```

The timing results for this procedure are as follows, where

N = file size
T = sorting time in milliseconds
A = $100T/(N \text{ LOG2}(N))$.

N=	1	2	4	7	11	18	29	46	72	114
T=	1.13	1.52	2.40	3.74	5.57	8.83	13.6	21.1	32.3	51.0
A=	113.	75.9	30.0	19.0	14.6	11.8	9.64	8.31	7.27	6.55

N=	179	280	439	686	1073
T=	79.2	124.	194.	302.	476.
A=	5.91	5.45	5.03	4.67	4.41

The storage required is 690 bytes plus 4n bytes for the two sorting bins.

_____
20. Downward Radix Sort.
_____

We illustrate the downward sort by a simple example using a binary radix. Given the file

(4 2 7 5 8 1 3 9 6),

start out by converting it to binary:

Internal Sorting
11. Sorting Methods.
    12. Integral Methods.
        20. Downward Radix Sort.

(0100 0010 0111 0101 1000 0001 0011 1001 0110).

Put the items into two bins; the lower bin contains the items for which the first digit is 0; the upper bin contains the items whose first digit is 1. The relative order of items within each bin is left unchanged:

(0100 0010 0111 0101 0001 0011 0110) (1000 1001).

Now divide each bin into a lower and upper part, using the second digit in the same way:

(0010 0001 0011) (0100 0111 0101 0110) (1000 1001).

Subdivide again, using the third digit:

(0001) (0010 0011) (0100 0101) (0111 0110) (1000 1001).

Subdivide again, using the fourth digit:

(0001) (0010) (0011) (0100) (0101) (0110) (0111) (1000) (1001).

The file is now order.
    A more general and somewhat more formal description of the process is as follows.
    Let K be an integral key mapping function whose maximum value is M. Let $r(1), r(2), \ldots, r(k)$ be a set of integers, each greater than 1, whose product is greater than or equal to M. The number $r(j)$ is called the j-th (descending) radix.
    Assign storage for $r(1)$ "bins", each bin containing locations into which file items can be put. Number these bins $0, 1, \ldots, r(1)-1$. Each bin is originally empty. Now for each item $X(1)$, $X(2), \ldots$ in turn compute $b(i) = [KX(i)/r(1)]$ and $K(1) X(i) = \text{MOD}(KX(i), r(1))$. Put the item $X(i)$ in the $b(i)$-th bin.
    Now, working recursively, sort each of these bins independently using the mapping function $K(1)$ and the radix $r(2)$. And so continue until the last set of bins has been sorted on the least significant radix $r(k)$.
    The file will then, when the bins are put one after the other, be in sort.
    The handling of the bins is usually done by tree-processing techniques; the trie memory (Fredkin 1960) represents a specific implementation.
    The sorting time, additional storage required, and conditions for suitability are comparable to the upward radix sort, for internal sorting.
    The downward radix sort is also well adapted to tape sorting, using one tape for each bin (at the current level).

Internal Sorting
11. Sorting Methods.
    12. Integral Methods.
        20. Downward Radix Sort.

A procedure for the downward binary radix sort is illustrated below. The logic for keeping track of the unsorted segments by means of a pushdown list is similar to that used for Quicksort (par. 55) except that the bit position to be used for partitioning the segment must also be recorded.

The procedure as written is not sequence-preserving.

```
SRT:    PROC(N); /* DESCENDING BINARY RADIX SORT */
        DCL (N,LL,UL,LI,UI,ML,Y) FIXED BIN(15);
        DCL (P,LV(20),UV(20),MV(20)) FIXED BIN(15);
        DCL M FIXED BIN(15);  /* CONVERSION SET */
        DCL B BIT(16) DEF M;
        P = 1;                    /* INITIALIZE PUSHDOWN LIST */
        LV(1) = 1;
        UV(1) = N;
        MV(1) = 2;
STB:    /* DO PARTITION OF ONE SEGMENT */
        IF P<1 THEN RETURN;
        LL = LV(P);
        UL = UV(P);
        ML = MV(P);
        IF UL-LL<1 THEN DO;
STD:      P = P - 1;
          GO TO STB;
          END;
        LI = LL - 1;
        UI = UL + 1;
STF:    IF UI-LI<2 THEN GO TO STL; /* TRY MOVING LI */
        LI = LI + 1;
        M = X(LI);
        IF ¬SUBSTR(B,ML,1) THEN GO TO STF;
STH:    IF UI-LI<2 THEN GO TO STJ; /* TRY MOVING UI */
        UI = UI - 1;
        M = X(UI);
        IF SUBSTR(B,ML,1) THEN GO TO STH;
        Y = X(LI);                /* INTERCHANGE ITEMS */
        X(LI) = X(UI);
        X(UI) = Y;
        GO TO STF;
STJ:    UI = UI - 1;
STL:    /* THE PARTITION IS COMPLETE. STORE BOTH SEGMENTS. */
        IF ML>=16 THEN GO TO STD;
        MV(P) = ML + 1;
        MV(P+1) = ML + 1;
        IF (UI-LL)<(UL-UI) THEN DO;
          LV(P+1) = LV(P);
          UV(P+1) = UI - 1;
          LV(P) = UI;
          END;
        ELSE DO;
```

Internal Sorting
11. Sorting Methods.
    12. Integral Methods.
        20. Downward Radix Sort.


```
        LV(P+1) = UI;
        UV(P+1) = UV(P);
        UV(P) = UI - 1;
        END;
     P = P + 1;
     GO TO STB;
     END SRT;
```

The timing results for this procedure are as follows, where

N = file size
T = sorting time in milliseconds
A = 100T/(N LOG2(N)).

N=	1	2	4	7	11	18	29	46	72	114
T=	.075	.426	.929	1.70	2.97	5.15	8.79	14.6	24.9	40.9
A=	7.54	21.3	11.6	8.64	7.80	6.86	6.23	5.74	5.61	5.26

N=	179	280	439	686	1073
T=	67.0	110.	181.	291.	472.
A=	5.00	4.83	4.71	4.50	4.37

The storage required for this procedure is 1276 bytes.

21. Matrix Method.

Gladun (1965) describes a radix method in which the bin bookeeping is done in a special matrix, with a variation to take account of equal keys.

22. Remarks.

The integral methods just described are quite appealing when the key mapping K is well adapted to their use, that is, when the numbers KX(i) are integers spread over an interval (1,M) without too many coincidences or gaps.

Unfortunately that condition does not hold for many key mappings of practical importance, and integral methods are not a good choice for a general purpose sorting routine.

We proceed, therefore, to non-integral methods, or comparative methods, in which the only requirement on the key mapping KX is that it permit the comparison of any two items to see which must precede the other.

Internal Sorting
11. Sorting Methods.
    12. Integral Methods.
        22. Remarks.

---

23. Merging.

Sorting by merging is the usual way of carrying out an external sort using serial files. The method is ordinarily attributed to Goldstine and von Neumann (1948). Mauchly presented it in a lecture in July 1946, though it was not published (Mauchly 1948) until later.

Many variations, designed to reduce the sorting time for an external sort, are discussed in the literature (see bibliography, par. 84), and are not further treated here. Iverson (1962, chapter 6) gives a useful summary.

A file segment X(a:b) is called a string if it is in sort, a maximal string if it is not part of a longer string. Two or more input strings may be merged to form a single output string; simply move to the output string, one at a time, the smallest item remaining in the input strings. Only the first remaining item in each input string need be checked to select the item to be moved.

If each set of p consecutive strings in a file is merged in this way, it is called a p-way merge pass over the file. A similar pass may then be made over the output, and the process may be continued until only a single string remains. The file is then in sort.

By breaking ties in favor of the item which was originally earlier in the file, we may ensure that the process is sequence preserving.

For internal sorting there seems to be no reason for choosing a value of p greater than 2; this is not the case for external sorting.

Various binary (or 2-way) merge methods may be distinguished by the way the initial strings are chosen.

Several of these different methods are next discussed.

24. Natural Merging.

If successive maximal strings are chosen, then we have a natural merge. For a random initial file of n items the average number of strings is (n+1)/2 (Friend 1956 p.136), so that the average string length is 2n/(n+1), or approximately 2 for large n. The actual lengths of the strings in a particular file may be quite variable.

An example of this process has been given in par. 11.

We start by a scan of the initial file to identify the existing consecutive maximal strings and distribute them alternately to the first pair of working files. Each string is followed by a marker item "-1", and the end of each of the two working files is marked by an end-of-file marker item "-2".

Internal Sorting
11. Sorting Methods.
    23. Merging.
       24. Natural Merging.

      The end-of-string markers (or some logical equivalent) are
necessary for sequence preservation. If the end of a string is
identified simply as a place where a larger item is followed (on
a work file) by a smaller item, then it could happen that what
were originally two separate strings would look like a single
string, and sequence would not necessarily be preserved.
      The strings are then merged from the first pair of work
files to the second, then from the second to the first, and so on
until only a single string remains. This final string is then
copied back to the original file space and the sort is complete.
      The procedure looks like this.

```
SRT:    PROC(N); /* NATURAL MERGE */
        DCL N FIXED BIN(15);   /* FILE SIZE */
        DCL Y(0:1,0:1,0:10002) FIXED BIN(15); /* WORK SPACE */
        DCL PS FIXED BIN(15); /* PHASE SWITCH */
        DCL OS FIXED BIN(15); /* OUTPUT FILE SWITCH */
        DCL OP(0:1) FIXED BIN(15); /* OUTPUT FILE POINTERS */
        DCL IP(0:1) FIXED BIN(15); /* INPUT POINTERS */
        DCL I FIXED BIN(15);
        Y(*,*,0) = -1;           /* INITIALIZE WORK SPACE */
        /* MAKE INITIAL SPLIT */
        OP = 1;                  /* OUTPUT FILE POINTERS */
        OS = 0;                  /* OUTPUT FILE SWITCH */
        DO I = 1 TO N;
          IF X(I)<Y(0,OS,OP(OS)-1) THEN DO;
            Y(0,OS,OP(OS)) = -1;
            OP(OS) = OP(OS) + 1;
            OS = 1 - OS;
            END;
          Y(0,OS,OP(OS)) = X(I);
          OP(OS) = OP(OS) + 1;
          END;
        Y(0,OS,OP(OS)) = -1;   /* END OF LAST STRING */
        OP(OS) = OP(OS) + 1;
        Y(0,0,OP(0)) = -2;     /* ENDS OF FILE */
        Y(0,1,OP(1)) = -2;
        PS = 0;                /* PHASE SWITCH */
 SRTB:  /* DO ONE MERGING PASS */
        IF Y(PS,1,1) = -2 THEN DO; /* TEST FOR THROUGH */
          DO I = 1 TO N;
            X(I) = Y(PS,0,I);
            END;
          RETURN;
          END;
        OS = 0;
        OP = 1;
        IP = 1;
 SRTD:  IF Y(PS,0,IP(0))<=Y(PS,1,IP(1)) THEN I=0;
                                        ELSE I=1;
```

Internal Sorting
11. Sorting Methods.
   23. Merging.
      24. Natural Merging.

```
IF Y(PS,I,IP(I))>-1 THEN DO;
   Y(1-PS,OS,OP(OS)) = Y(PS,I,IP(I));
   OP(OS) = OP(OS) + 1;
   IP(I) = IP(I) + 1;
   GO TO SRTD;
   END;
I = 1 - I;
DO WHILE(Y(PS,I,IP(I))>-1); /* FINISH STRING */
   Y(1-PS,OS,OP(OS)) = Y(PS,I,IP(I));
   OP(OS) = OP(OS) + 1;
   IP(I) = IP(I) + 1;
   END;
Y(1-PS,OS,OP(OS)) = -1; /* WRITE END OF STRING */
OP(OS) = OP(OS) + 1;
OS = 1 - OS;                /* SWITCH OUTPUT FILES */
IF Y(PS,0,IP(0))=-1 THEN IP(0) = IP(0) + 1;
IF Y(PS,1,IP(1))=-1 THEN IP(1) = IP(1) + 1;
IF (Y(PS,0,IP(0))>-1)|(Y(PS,1,IP(1))>-1) THEN GO TO SRTD;
PS = 1 - PS;               /* END THIS MERGE PASS */
Y(PS,0,OP(0)) = -2;
Y(PS,1,OP(1)) = -2;
GO TO SRTB;
END SRT;
```

The timing results are as follows, where

N = file size
T = sorting time in milliseconds
A = $100T/(N\ LOG2(N))$
C = number of comparisons
R = number of replacements
A superscript means multiplication by that power of 10.

N=	1	2	4	7	11	18	29	46	72	114
T=	.671	.749	.955	1.27	1.80	2.73	4.11	7.08	12.2	19.2
A=	67.1	37.4	11.9	6.45	4.74	3.63	2.92	2.79	2.74	2.47
C=	2.00	9.60	28.0	53.9	93.8	165.	265.	460.	781.	1220
R=	5.00	10.6	23.4	43.8	74.6	133.	218.	382.	659.	1042

N=	179	280	439	686	1073	1677	2621	4096	6400	10000
T=	32.9	57.6	89.8	154.	266.	416.	706.	1153	1879	3130
A=	2.45	2.53	2.33	2.38	2.46	2.32	2.37	2.35	2.32	2.36
C=	2091	3549	5510	9319	1560^1	2435^1	4067^1	6583^1	1057^2	1751^2
R=	1809	3104	4846	8260	1397^1	2182^1	3672^1	5963^1	9604^1	1600^2

The storage required is 1830 + 8n bytes.

Internal Sorting
11. Sorting Methods.
    23. Merging.
        25. Straight Merging.

----
25. Straight Merging.

In straight, or pure, merging, we start with initial strings
of length one. That is, in the first pass, the odd numbered items
of the initial file are sent to one output (working file) and the
even numbered items to the other. These strings of length one are
merged, in the second pass, to form strings of length two in the
other pair of working files. And so on, until a single string
consisting of the whole file is obtained.
If we start, for example, with the file

    (4 1 2 7 5 8 1 3 9 6)

and mark off strings of length one we get

    ([4][1][2][7][5][8][1][3][9][6]).

Merging successive pairs of strings gives

    ([1 4][2 7][5 8][1 3][6 9])
    ([1 2 4 7][1 3 5 8][6 9])
    ([1 1 2 3 4 5 7 8][6 9])
    [1 1 2 3 4 5 6 7 8 9].

This is the method described by Goldstine and von Neumann
(1948).
Starting out with all strings of the same length has the
advantage that at the beginning of any merging pass, all strings
(except perhaps the last) are of the same length, so that string
locations can be kept track of by arithmetic rather than by
pointers or markers.
The straight merge procedure looks like this.

```
SRT:    PROC(N); /* MERGE: INITIAL STRINGS OF LENGTH 1 */
        DCL(N,Z(10000),Y,I,J,L,M,LL,LU,UL,UU)
            FIXED BIN(15);
        L = 1;
SRTD:   /* MERGE FROM X TO Z */
        IF L>=N THEN RETURN;
        M = 1;                  /* POINTER TO Z */
        DO I = 1 BY 2*L TO N;
            LL = I;             /* LOW SEGMENT POINTER */
            LU = MIN(N,I+L-1);  /* LOW SEGMENT BOUND */
            UL = I + L - 1;     /* UPPER SEGMENT POINTER */
            UU = MIN(N,I+2*L-1); /* UPPER SEGMENT BOUND */
SRTF:       /* STEP UPPER POINTER */
            UL = UL + 1;
            IF UL<=UU THEN GO TO SRTJ;
            DO J = LL TO LU;
```

Internal Sorting
11. Sorting Methods.
     23. Merging.
          25. Straight Merging.

```
                Z(M) = X(J);
                M = M + 1;
                END;
           GO TO SRTL;
SRTH:      /* STEP LOWER POINTER */
           LL = LL + 1;
           IF LL<=LU THEN GO TO SRTJ;
           DO J = UL TO UU;
              Z(M) = X(J);
              M = M + 1;
              END;
           GO TO SRTL;
SRTJ:      /* MAKE THE COMPARISON */
           IF X(LL) <=X(UL) THEN DO;
              Z(M) = X(LL);
              M = M + 1;
              GO TO SRTH;
              END;
           Z(M) = X(UL);
           M = M + 1;
           GO TO SRTF;
SRTL:      END;
           L = 2*L;                    /* DOUBLE STRING LENGTH */
SRTN:  /* MERGE FROM Z TO X */
       IF L>=N THEN DO;               /* TEST FOR MERGE COMPLETE */
           DO I = 1 TO N;
              X(I) = Z(I);
              END;
           RETURN;
           END;
       M = 1;                          /* POINTER TO X */
       DO I = 1 BY 2*L TO N;
           LL = I;
           LU = MIN(N,I+L-1);
           UL = I + L - 1;
           UU = MIN(N,I+2*L-1);
SRTP:      /* STEP UPPER POINTER */
           UL = UL + 1;
           IF UL<=UU THEN GO TO SRTT;
           DO J = LL TO LU;
              X(M) = Z(J);
              M = M + 1;
              END;
           GO TO SRTV;
SRTR:      /* MOVE LOWER POINTER */
           LL = LL + 1;
           IF LL<=LU THEN GO TO SRTT;
           DO J = UL TO UU;
              X(M) = Z(J);
              M = M + 1;
```

Internal Sorting
11. Sorting Methods.
    23. Merging.
        25. Straight Merging.


```
            END;
            GO TO SRTV;
SRTT:       /* MAKE THE COMPARISON */
            IF Z(LL)<=Z(UL) THEN DO;
              X(M) = Z(LL);
              M = M + 1;
              GO TO SRTR;
              END;
            X(M) = Z(UL);
            M = M + 1;
            GO TO SRTP;
SRTV:       END;
            L = 2*L;                    /* DOUBLE THE STRING LENGTH */
            GO TO SRTD;
            END SRT;
```

The timing results were as follows, where

N = file size
T = sorting time in milliseconds
A = 100T/(N LOG2(N))
C = number of comparisons
R = number of replacements.
A superscript means multiplication by that power of 10.

N=	1	2	4	7	11	18	29	46	72	114
T=	.426	.489	.541	.765	1.03	1.56	2.22	3.40	6.18	9.50
A=	42.6	24.4	6.77	3.89	2.71	2.08	1.58	1.34	1.39	1.22
C=	0.00	1.00	4.67	12.6	26.8	58.4	106.	203.	386.	644.
R=	0.00	4.00	8.00	28.0	44.0	108.	174.	276.	576.	912.

N=	179	280	439	686	1073	1677	2621	4096	6400	10000
T=	15.2	26.9	42.4	70.0	122.	187.	301.	484.	826.	1332
A=	1.13	1.18	1.10	1.08	1.13	1.04	1.01	.984	1.02	1.00
C=	1145	2077	3336	5754	1021^1	1614^1	2737^1	4398^1	7433^1	1237^2
R=	1432	2800	4390	6860	1288^1	2012^1	3145^1	4915^1	8960^1	1400^2

The storage required is 1602 + 2n bytes.
The procedure as written is sequence-preserving.

26. Optimal Initial Strings.

In the above procedure we started out by building fixed-length strings of length L = 1 before the first merge pass. Let us now discuss alternative choices of L. If we sort (n/L) strings of length L by ranking (par. 45) and then merge these strings, the number of comparisons is approximately

$$C(L) = (n/L)L(L-1)/4 + n \, LOG2(n/L),$$

Internal Sorting
11. Sorting Methods.
    23. Merging.
        26. Optimal Initial Strings.

ignoring the distinction between real and integer arithmetic.
This function takes its minimum at L = 4/(ln 2) = 5.78. On this
rough basis, then, one might choose L as either 5 or 6. But, as
the program shows, the ranking comparisons are made in a tighter
loop (i.e., with less overhead) than the merging comparisons,
indicating a larger choice of L.
      Also, one might choose a particular value of L for a given n
so that the initial number of strings is just less than or equal
to a power of two for further efficiency. The resulting procedure
looks like this.

```
SRT:   PROC(N); /* MERGE: OPTIMAL INITIAL STRINGS */
       DCL(N,Z(10000),Y,I,J,L,M,LL,LU,UL,UU)
         FIXED BIN(15);
       I = N/6;        /* FIND INITIAL STRING LENGTH */
       J = 1;
       DO WHILE(J<I);
         J = J + J;
         END;
       L = N/J;
       IF L*J<N THEN L = L + 1;
       DO M = 1 BY L TO N-1; /* SORT INITIAL STRINGS */
         DO J = M TO MIN(N,M+L-1)-1;
           Y = X(J+1);
           DO I = J BY -1 TO M WHILE(Y<X(I));
             X(I+1) = X(I);
             END;
           X(I+1) = Y;
           END;
         END;
SRTD:  /* MERGE FROM X TO Z */
       IF L>=N THEN RETURN;
       M = 1;                     /* POINTER TO Z */
       DO I = 1 BY 2*L TO N;
         LL = I;                  /* LOW SEGMENT POINTER */
         LU = MIN(N,I+L-1);   /* LOW SEGMENT BOUND */
         UL = I + L - 1;       /* UPPER SEGMENT POINTER */
         UU = MIN(N,I+2*L-1); /* UPPER SEGMENT BOUND */
SRTF:    /* STEP UPPER POINTER */
         UL = UL + 1;
         IF UL<=UU THEN GO TO SRTJ;
         DO J = LL TO LU;
           Z(M) = X(J);
           M = M + 1;
           END;
         GO TO SRTL;
SRTH:    /* STEP LOWER POINTER */
         LL = LL + 1;
         IF LL<=LU THEN GO TO SRTJ;
         DO J = UL TO UU;
```

Internal Sorting
11. Sorting Methods.
    23. Merging.
        26. Optimal Initial Strings.

```
           Z(M) = X(J);
           M = M + 1;
           END;
         GO TO SRTL;
 SRTJ:   /* MAKE THE COMPARISON */
         IF X(LL)<=X(UL) THEN DO;
           Z(M) = X(LL);
           M = M + 1;
           GO TO SRTH;
           END;
         Z(M) = X(UL);
         M = M + 1;
         GO TO SRTF;
 SRTL:   END;
         L = 2*L;                     /* DOUBLE STRING LENGTH */
 SRTN: /* MERGE FROM Z TO X */
         IF L>=N THEN DO;             /* TEST FOR MERGE COMPLETE */
           DO I = 1 TO N;
             X(I) = Z(I);
             END;
           RETURN;
           END;
         M = 1;                       /* POINTER TO X */
         DO I = 1 BY 2*L TO N;
           LL = I;
           LU = MIN(N,I+L-1);
           UL = I + L - 1;
           UU = MIN(N,I+2*L-1);
 SRTP:   /* STEP UPPER POINTER */
           UL = UL + 1;
           IF UL<=UU THEN GO TO SRTT;
           DO J = LL TO LU;
             X(M) = Z(J);
             M = M + 1;
             END;
         GO TO SRTV;
 SRTR:   /* MOVE LOWER POINTER */
           LL = LL + 1;
           IF LL<=LU THEN GO TO SRTT;
           DO J = UL TO UU;
             X(M) = Z(J);
             M = M + 1;
             END;
         GO TO SRTV;
 SRTT:   /* MAKE THE COMPARISON */
           IF Z(LL)<=Z(UL) THEN DO;
             X(M) = Z(LL);
             M = M + 1;
             GO TO SRTR;
             END;
```

Internal Sorting
11. Sorting Methods.
    23. Merging.
        26. Optimal Initial Strings.

```
          X(M) = Z(UL);
          M = M + 1;
          GO TO SRTP;
SRTV:     END;
          L = 2*L;                    /* DOUBLE THE STRING LENGTH */
          GO TO SRTD;
          END SRT;
```

The timing results were as follows, where

N = file size
T = sorting time in milliseconds
A = $100T/(N\ LOG2(N))$
C = number of comparisons
R = number of replacements.
A superscript means multiplication by that power of 10.

N=	1	2	4	7	11	18	29	46	72	114
T=	.416	.468	.489	.572	.752	1.08	1.63	2.68	4.28	7.70
A=	41.6	23.4	6.11	2.91	1.98	1.44	1.16	1.06	.965	.988
C=	0.00	1.60	6.15	15.9	39.2	60.8	125.	218.	388.	681.
R=	0.00	2.60	9.15	21.9	49.2	71.4	141.	292.	399.	828.

N=	179	280	439	686	1073	1677	2621	4096	6400	10000
T=	12.0	19.7	35.5	56.6	92.1	162.	258.	421.	732.	1136
A=	.896	.865	.921	.875	.853	.904	.868	.856	.904	.855
C=	1199	2047	3482	5990	9976	1669^1	2788^1	4534^1	7647^1	1243^2
R=	1421	2008	3836	6459	9257	1709^1	2850^1	4024^1	7492^1	1214^2

The storage required is 2122 + 2n bytes.
The method as written is sequence-preserving.

27. Chain Merging.

This method is a formalization of the Patience Sort, attributed by Mallows (1962) to A.S.C. Ross.
We define a <u>chain</u> of items of a file X(1:n) to be any subsequence which is already in sort. Thus if i(1), i(2), ..., i(j), ..., i(J) is any increasing sequence of integers such that $KX(i(j)) \leq KX(i(j+1))$ for all j<J then this sequence of subscripts defines a chain.
The chain-merge sorting method divides the items of the file into several chains and then merges these chains by pairs until the file is in sort.
Start the first (oldest) chain with the item X(1). If $KX(1) \leq KX(2)$ then add X(2) to the tail of this first chain; otherwise start a second chain with X(2) as its head. And so continue, taking each file item in turn; add the item to the tail of the oldest chain it will fit on; if it is smaller than the tail item of every existing chain then start a new chain with it.

Internal Sorting
11. Sorting Methods.
    23. Merging.
        27. Chain Merging.

Applying this method to the file

(4 2 7 5 8 1 3 9 6),

for example, yields the chains

[4 7 8 9][2 5 6][1 3].

Merging the two shortest chains gives

[4 7 8 9][1 2 3 5 6],

and a final merge gives

[1 2 3 4 5 6 7 8 9].

The tail-items of the chains will then always be in monotone decreasing order, so that a binary search may be used to see where each new item goes.

The process is conveniently carried out using a predecessor vector $P(1:n)$ and a tail vector $T(1:d)$. $P(i)$ points to the predecessor of $X(i)$ within its chain; if $X(i)$ is the head of its chain then $P(i)=0$. $T(j)$ points to the tail item $X(T(j))$ of the j-th chain.

If at any point the number of chains required exceeds the number d of chains allowed for, then two older chains are merged to make room for the new one.

When every item of the file has been put in a chain in this way, the chains are merged. In the sample program, we choose the two consecutive chains with the smallest total length to be merged at each step.

When all chains have been merged into a single chain, the items are copied to a file $Z(1:n)$ in the correct order: tail of the chain to $Z(n)$, its predecessor to $Z(n-1)$, and so on. Then, finally, the sorted file Z is copied back into X and the sort is complete.

This method requires additional storage for $Z(1:n)$, $P(1:n)$ and $T(1:d)$. Its timing function is of order $n \log n$.

The method is sequence-preserving if merging is always done on adjacent chains and ties are broken in the correct direction, as in the test procedure shown below.

The method is quite sensitive to existing order in the original file. It takes excellent advantage of positive bias, at the cost of poor performance in the presence of negative bias.

Internal Sorting
11. Sorting Methods.
    23. Merging.
        27. Chain Merging.

It is important to allow the right amount d of storage for the tail-pointer vector $T(1:d)$, and the dependence of d on the file length n is therefore of interest. Mallows points out that, for a given file, the number of chains generated is equal to the length of the longest monotone properly decreasing subsequence of file items. This number clearly ranges from 1 (file initially in sort order) to n (file initially in the reverse of sort order). The question of the length of the longest subsequence has been investigated by Baer (1962) and Schensted (1961) as well as by Mallows, but not in a way that helps much in the present context.

Experiment indicates that if d chains are allowed for a random file of fewer than $d^2/2$ items then the timing will not be adversely affected very often.

The test procedure used for the timing runs was as follows.

```
SRT:    PROC(N); /* SORT BY CHAINS */
        DCL C FIXED BIN(15)INIT(0); /* NUMBER OF CHAINS */
        DCL (I,J,K,JL,JU)FIXED BIN(15); /* TEMPOS */
        DCL L(1000)FIXED BIN(15); /* LENGTHS OF CHAINS */
        DCL MER ENTRY(FIXED BIN(15)); /* MERGE TWO CHAINS */
        DCL MI FIXED BIN(15) INIT(1); /* MERGE INDEX */
        DCL MJ FIXED BIN(15) INIT(0); /* PHASER */
        DCL N FIXED BIN(15); /* FILE LENGTH */
        DCL P(10000)FIXED BIN(15); /* PREDECESSOR POINTERS */
        DCL T(1000)FIXED BIN(15); /* TAIL POINTERS */
        DCL Z(10000)FIXED BIN(15); /* COPY OF FILE */
        /* BUILD UP THE CHAINS */
        DO I = 1 TO N;          /* ADD EACH ITEM */
          JL = 0;               /* BINARY SEARCH */
          JU = C + 1;
          DO WHILE(JU-JL>1);
            J = (JU+JL)/2;
            IF X(I)>=X(T(J)) THEN JU = J;
                             ELSE JL = J;

            END;
          IF JU>C THEN DO;      /* TEST FOR NEW CHAIN */
            IF C>=1000 THEN DO; /* TEST OVERFLOW */
              CALL MER(MI);
              MI = 1 + MOD(MI,998);
              JU = JU - 1;
              END;
            T(JU) = 0;
            L(JU) = 0;
            C = C + 1;
            END;
          P(I) = T(JU);         /* ADD ITEM TO CHAIN */
          T(JU) = I;
          L(JU) = L(JU) + 1;
          END;
        /* THE CHAINS HAVE BEEN BUILT. MERGE BY PAIRS. */
```

Internal Sorting
11. Sorting Methods.
    23. Merging.
        27. Chain Merging.

```
DO WHILE(C>1);
  J = 1;  /* FIND SMALLEST ADJACENT PAIR OF CHAINS */
  K = L(1) + L(2);
  DO I = 2 TO C-1;
    IF L(I)+L(I+1)<K THEN DO;
      J = I;
      K = L(I) + L(I+1);
      END;
    END;
  CALL MER(J); /* MERGE THE TWO SMALL CHAINS */
  END;
/* THERE IS NOW A SINGLE CHAIN. COLLECT IT IN Z. */
J = T(1);
DO I = N BY -1 TO 1;
  Z(I) = X(J);
  J = P(J);
  END;
/* NOW COPY BACK TO X. */
DO I = 1 TO N;
  X(I) = Z(I);
  END;
RETURN;
MER:    PROC(I); /* MERGE TWO ADJACENT CHAINS */
DCL (I,J) FIXED BIN(15); /* CHAIN NUMBERS */
DCL (T1,T2) FIXED BIN(15); /* CURRENT TAILS, OLD CHAINS */
DCL H FIXED BIN(15); /* CURRENT HEAD OF NEW CHAIN */
DCL K FIXED BIN(15); /* TEMPO */
J = I + 1;
H = T(I);
T1 = P(H);
T2 = T(J);
DO WHILE(T1*T2>0);
  IF X(T1)<=X(T2) THEN DO;
    P(H) = T2;
    H = T2;
    T2 = P(T2);
    END;
  ELSE DO;
    P(H) = T1;
    H = T1;
    T1 = P(T1);
    END;
  END;
P(H) = MAX(T1,T2);
/* THE CHAINS ARE MERGED. FINISH UP. */
L(I) = L(I) + L(J);    /* CORRECT COUNT */
DO K = J TO C-1;       /* CLOSE UP TAIL POINTERS */
  T(K) = T(K+1);
  L(K) = L(K+1);
  END;
```

Internal Sorting
11. Sorting Methods.
   23. Merging.
      27. Chain Merging.

```
      C = C - 1;                    /* CORRECT CHAIN COUNT */
      RETURN;
      END MER;
      END SRT;
```

The timing results for this procedure are as follows, where

N = file size
T = sorting time in milliseconds
A = $100T/(N\ LOG2(N))$
C = number of comparisons
R = number of replacements.
A superscript means multiplication by that power of 10.

N=	1	2	4	7	11	18	29	46	72	114
T=	.444	.525	.652	.869	1.22	1.84	2.95	4.74	7.45	12.7
A=	44.4	26.2	8.16	4.42	3.21	2.46	2.09	1.87	1.68	1.63
C=	0.00	1.00	5.40	15.3	32.5	69.0	138.	257.	452.	826.
R=	2.00	4.00	8.00	14.0	22.0	36.0	58.0	92.0	144.	228.

N=	179	280	439	686	1073	1677	2621	4096	6400	10000
T=	21.0	34.3	56.0	92.6	151.	248.	403.	655.	1070	1738
A=	1.57	1.51	1.45	1.43	1.40	1.38	1.35	1.33	1.32	1.31
C=	1446	2469	4176	7056	1175^1	1964^1	3255^1	5363^1	8821^1	1447^2
R=	358.	560.	878.	1372	2146	3354	5242	8192	1280^1	2000^1

The storage required for this procedure is 1852 bytes plus 2n for the predecessor vector, 2n for the second copy of the file, 2d for the tail pointers, and 2d for the chain lengths: a total of 45,852 for the procedure shown.

---
28. Ancestral Sorting.

This method arranges the items in a binary tree, but by a different method than the Treesort procedure described in par. 65.

To apply this method to the file

(4 2 7 5 8 1 3 9 6),

for example, we start by taking the first item as the root of the tree:

    4.

Since the second item is smaller, we make it a left branch:

```
        4
      ┌─┘
      2
```

Since the third item is larger, we make it a right branch:

The fourth item is added as follows:

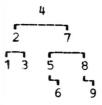

and so on, until the final tree takes the form

```
          4
     ┌────────┐
     2        7
  ┌──┐     ┌──┐
  1  3     5  8
            └┐  └┐
             6   9
```

An actual computer procedure may be developed as follows.
A pointer matrix P(n,3) is used, with one row for each item of the file, to store the information for the corresponding node of the binary tree. For the i-th node, P(i,1) points to the father, P(i,2) to the smaller son, and P(i,3) to the larger son. If any of these three relatives does not exist, then the corresponding pointer is zero.
Thus P(1,1)=0 since the root of the tree (corresponding to the first item of the file) has no father. If P(i,2) = P(i,3) = 0 then the i-th node has no sons and is called a 'terminal node' or 'leaf'. The tree is constructed so that

$$KX(P(i,2)) < KX(i) \text{ if } P(i,2) > 0,$$
$$KX(i) \leq KX(P(i,3)) \text{ if } P(i,3) > 0;$$

so that the item corresponding to the i-th node lies between the two sons of that node (in the sorting sequence), providing the sons exist.
The sort proceeds in three steps:

1) The tree is built,
2) Items are copied into an array Z(1:n) in the order specified by the tree,
3) Z is copied back into X.

At the beginning of the sort all nodes are empty. Each item

Internal Sorting
11. Sorting Methods.
    28. Ancestral Sorting.

in turn has its node fastened to the tree by tracing the branches
of that part of the tree that is already built.
    The details are best understood from the program itself,
which is as follows.

```
SRT:    PROC(N); /* ANCESTRAL SORT */
        DCL P(10000,3) FIXED BIN(15); /* POINTER ARRAY:
                            P(J,1) POINTS TO FATHER
                            P(J,2) POINTS TO SMALLER SON
                            P(J,3) POINTS TO LARGER SON */
        DCL Z(10000) FIXED BIN(15); /* COPY OF FILE */
        DCL (I,N,Q) FIXED BIN(15);
        /* BUILD THE TREE. */
        DO I = 1 TO N;
          P(I,*) = 0;               /* POINTERS TO ZERO */
          Q = 1;                    /* SET NODE POINTER */
          DO WHILE(Q<I);
            IF X(I)<X(Q) THEN J = 2; /* CHOOSE SON */
                          ELSE J = 3;
            IF P(Q,J)>0 THEN Q = P(Q,J);
            ELSE DO;               /* SON DOES NOT EXIST */
              P(Q,J) = I;
              P(I,1) = Q;
              Q = I;
              END;
            END;
          END;
        /* THE TREE IS BUILT. UNBUILD IT INTO Z. */
        I = 0;                      /* POINTER TO Z */
        Q = 1;                      /* ACTIVE NODE */
        DO WHILE(I<N);
          IF P(Q,2)>0 THEN Q = P(Q,2); /* TAKE SMALL SON */
          ELSE DO;
            I = I + 1;
            Z(I) = X(Q);
            IF P(Q,1)=0 THEN DO; /* TEST FOR ROOT */
              IF P(Q,3)=0 THEN;  /* TEST FOR TERMINAL */
              ELSE DO;
                Q = P(Q,3);
                P(Q,1) = 0;
                END;
              END;
            ELSE DO; /* NOT A ROOT */
              IF P(P(Q,1),2)=Q THEN J = 2;
                              ELSE J = 3;
              IF P(Q,3)>0 THEN P(P(Q,3),1) = P(Q,1);
              P(P(Q,1),J) = P(Q,3);
              Q = P(Q,1);
              END;
            END;
          END;
```

Internal Sorting
11. Sorting Methods.
    28. Ancestral Sorting.

```
      /* THE SORTED FILE IS IN Z. COPY TO X. */
      DO I = 1 TO N;
        X(I) = Z(I);
        END;
      RETURN;
      END SRT;
```

The timing results for this procedure are as follows, where

N = file size
T = sorting time in milliseconds
A = 100T(N LOG2(N))
C = number of comparisons
R = number of replacements.
A superscript means multiplication by that power of 10.

N=	1	2	4	7	11	18	29	46	72	114
T=	.489	.554	.703	.924	1.29	2.02	3.29	5.44	8.85	15.2
A=	48.9	27.7	8.78	4.70	3.39	2.69	2.34	2.14	1.99	1.95
C=	0.00	1.00	4.90	14.2	27.9	62.3	123.	227.	409.	782.
R=	2.00	4.00	8.00	14.0	22.0	36.0	58.0	92.0	144.	228.

N=	179	280	439	686	1073	1677	2621	4096	6400	10000
T=	25.1	41.6	68.5	111.	183.	305.	500.	822.	1359	2213
A=	1.87	1.83	1.78	1.71	1.70	1.70	1.68	1.67	1.68	1.67
C=	1377	2401	4128	6936	1181^1	2024^1	3395^1	5675^1	9356^1	1548^2
R=	358.	560.	878.	1372	2146	3354	5242	8192	1280^1	2000^1

The method is sequence-preserving and of order n log n for random files. It is sensitive to order, being of timing order n^2 for files initially in sort, as programmed above, and this disadvantage is difficult to overcome by modification of the program.

MacLaughlin (1963) suggests a method for keeping the branches of the tree of almost equal lengths.

The storage required is 1058 bytes plus 6n for the pointers and 2n for the second copy of the file, or 81,058 total for the procedure shown.

_____
29. Use of Based Variables.
_____

The procedure in par. 28 handles the pointers explicitly. Mrs. Jane Olmer has provided the procedure below, which uses based variables for tree management, and also allocates storage only as it is needed.

The procedure is as follows.

```
 SRT:   PROC(N); /* ANCESTRAL SORT, BASED VARIABLES */
        DCL 1 TREE BASED(PTREE),
              2 Z FIXED BIN(15),           /* ITEM FROM VECTOR */
              2 BACK POINTER,
              2 UP POINTER,
```

Internal Sorting
11. Sorting Methods.
    28. Ancestral Sorting.
       29. Use of Based Variables.

```
      2 DOWN POINTER;
  DCL (PTREE,PTREE1,PT) POINTER;
  DCL (I,N) FIXED BIN(15);
  ALLOCATE TREE;                      /* STORE INITIAL ITEM */
  PTREE1 = PTREE;
  Z = X(1);
  BACK, UP, DOWN = NULL;
  DO I = 2 TO N;
    ALLOCATE TREE;                    /* ADD NEXT ITEM */
    Z = X(I);
    BACK, UP, DOWN = NULL;
    PT = PTREE1;
    DO WHILE (BACK = NULL);           /* SCAN TREE FOR FATHER */
    IF Z < PT->Z THEN DO;
      IF PT->DOWN = NULL THEN DO;
        PT->DOWN = PTREE;
        BACK = PT;
        END;
      ELSE PT = PT->DOWN;
      END;
    ELSE /* Z >= PT->Z */ DO;
      IF PT->UP = NULL THEN DO;
        PT->UP = PTREE;
        BACK = PT;
        END;
      ELSE PT = PT->UP;
      END;
    END;
    END;
  I = 0;
  PTREE = PTREE1;
  DO WHILE (I < N);
    IF DOWN = NULL THEN DO;
      I = I + 1;
      X(I) = Z;
      DO WHILE (UP = NULL);
        IF BACK = NULL THEN DO;
          FREE TREE;
          RETURN;                     /* EXIT FROM SRT */
          END;
        PT = PTREE;
        PTREE =BACK;
        FREE PT->TREE;
        IF DOWN ¬= NULL THEN DO;
          I = I + 1;
          X(I) = Z;
          DOWN = NULL;
          END;
        ELSE UP = NULL;
        END;
```

Internal Sorting
11. Sorting Methods.
    28. Ancestral Sorting.
        29. Use of Based Variables.


```
        PT = PTREE;
        PTREE = UP;
        BACK = PT->BACK;
        FREE PT->TREE;
        END;
      ELSE PTREE = DOWN;
      END;
    END SRT;
```

The timing results were as follows, where

N = file size
T = sorting time in milliseconds
A = 100T/(N LOG2(N)).

N=	1	2	4	7	11	18	29	46	72	114
T=	.294	.562	1.01	1.80	2.83	4.75	7.80	12.9	21.1	35.1
A=	29.4	28.1	12.6	9.18	7.44	6.33	5.54	5.08	4.76	4.51

N=	179	280	439	686	1073
T=	56.3	91.9	152.	251.	417.
A=	4.20	4.04	3.95	3.88	3.86

The amount of storage required is 1068 + 16n bytes.

----
30. Counting.

In this method (Friend 1956 p. 152) a count vector $C(1:n)$ is set to 1 at the beginning of the sort. Each item in turn is compared with each of the items that precede it in the file. Whichever of the two items is larger (or the later, in case of a tie) has the corresponding counter increased by one.

At end of this pass, the counter $C(j)$ for the j-th item will contain one plus the number of items less than or equal to $X(j)$ so that $C(j)$ is the rank of $X(j)$ in the sorted file.

This method is sequence-preserving, of order n^2, and requires additional storage for the rank vector $C(j)$.

In any method which produces a rank vector, the actual items may be put in order in either of two ways:

1) by using a second copy of the file (par. 31)
2) by successive interchanges (par. 32).

----
31. Use of a Second Copy of the File.

Once the rank vector $C(j)$ has been determined, each item $X(i)$ may be copied to the indicated location $Z(C(i))$ in a second copy Z of the file, and the file Z then copied back to X to complete the sort.

The procedure looks like this.

Internal Sorting
11. Sorting Methods.
    30. Counting.
        31. Use of a Second Copy of the File.


```
SRT:    PROC(N); /* SORT BY COUNTING */
        DCL (C(10000),Z(10000),N,I,J) FIXED BIN(15);
        DO I = 1 TO N;              /* SET THE COUNTS */
          C(I) = 1;
          DO J = 1 TO I-1;
            IF X(J)<=X(I) THEN C(I) = C(I) + 1;
                          ELSE C(J) = C(J) + 1;
          END;
        END;
        DO I = 1 TO N;              /* COPY TO Z */
          Z(C(I)) = X(I);
        END;
        DO I = 1 TO N;              /* COPY BACK TO X */
          X(I) = Z(I);
        END;
        RETURN;
        END SRT;
```

The timing results for this procedure are as follows, where

N = file size
T = sorting time in milliseconds
A = $100T/(n \ LOG2(N))$
C = number of comparisons
R = number of replacements.
A superscript means multiplication by that power of 10.

N=	1	2	4	7	11	18	29	46	72	114
T=	.450	.458	.531	.648	.913	1.62	3.34	7.46	17.1	41.9
A=	45.0	22.9	6.64	3.29	2.40	2.15	2.37	2.94	3.85	5.38
C=	0.00	1.00	6.00	21.0	55.0	153.	406.	1035	2556	6441
R=	2.00	4.00	8.00	14.0	22.0	36.0	58.0	92.0	144.	228.

N=	179	280	439	686	1073
T=	102.	249.	619.	1507	3627
A=	7.60	11.0	16.1	23.3	33.6
C=	1593^1	3906^1	96141	23502^2	57512^2
R=	358.	560.	878.	1372	2146

The storage required is 590 bytes plus 4n bytes for the counting vector and second copy of the file.

32. Successive Interchanges.

The additional storage for a second copy of the file may be saved, at the cost of extra computing time, by interchanging items (and their respective ranks) until each item is in the right location.
The procedure looks like this.

Internal Sorting
11. Sorting Methods.
    30. Counting.
       32. Successive Interchanges.


```
SRT:   PROC(N); /* COUNTING AND INTERCHANGE */
       DCL (C(10000),N,I,J,Y) FIXED BIN(15);
       DO I = 1 TO N;          /* SET THE COUNTS */
         C(I) = 1;
         DO J = 1 TO I-1;
           IF X(J)<=X(I) THEN C(I) = C(I) + 1;
                         ELSE C(J) = C(J) + 1;
         END;
       END;
       DO I = 1 TO N;          /* INTERCHANGE */
         DO WHILE(I¬=C(I));
           J = C(C(I));
           Y = X(C(I));
           C(C(I)) = C(I);
           X(C(I)) = X(I);
           C(I) = J;
           X(I) = Y;
         END;
       END;
       RETURN;
       END SRT;
```

The timing results are as follows, where

N = file size
T = sorting time in milliseconds
A = 100T/(N LOG2(N))
C = number of comparisons
R = number of replacements.
A superscript means multiplication by that power of 10.

N=	1	2	4	7	11	18	29	46	72	114
T=	.408	.429	.509	.661	.991	1.82	3.82	8.73	20.0	48.7
A=	40.8	21.4	6.37	3.36	2.60	2.42	2.71	3.43	4.51	6.26
C=	0.00	1.00	6.00	21.0	55.0	153.	406.	1035	2556	6441
R=	0.00	1.65	6.30	12.8	23.5	42.7	74.1	126.	200.	326.

N=	179	280	439	686	1073
T=	120.	287.	699.	1722	4263
A=	8.96	12.6	18.1	26.6	39.5
C=	15931^1	39061^1	96141^1	23502^2	57512^2
R=	520.	820.	1298	2035	3194

The storage required is 634 bytes plus the amount needed for the rank vector.
The method is sequence-preserving.

---
33. Selection Sorting.

Selection sorting, like the minima sort (par. 44) selects the smallest item in the file, then the next smallest, and so on. It differs from the minima sort, however, in that information is preserved from one selection to the next so that fewer comparisons are required.

This information is preserved in the form of a tree. Using a direct binary tree for this purpose (as in par. 36) on the file

(4 2 7 5 8 1 3 9 6)

would give an initial complete binary tree of the form

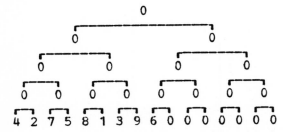

where the file items are put in the first n nodes of the highest level (as leaves) and the other nodes are 0 to show that they are not yet occupied. Now the smaller leaf in each pair is moved to the next level, and its original node is set to zero:

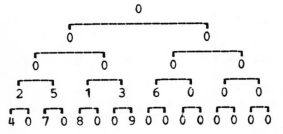

Now the smaller of each pair at the fourth level is moved down to the third level, and is replaced by its son:

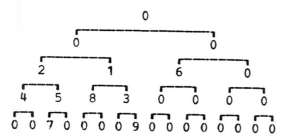

The smaller of each pair at the third level is moved down to the
second level, and replacements are made, as available, from the
higher levels:

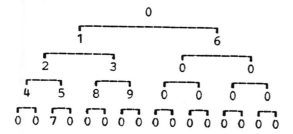

The smaller of the pair at the second level is moved down to the
first level, and replacements are made from the higher levels as
before:

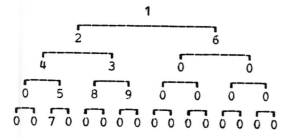

The smallest item in the file is now at the root of the
tree. It is copied to an output file, and replacements are made
from higher levels as before:

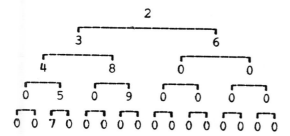

Internal Sorting
11. Sorting Methods.
   33. Selection Sorting.

   The next-to-smallest item is now at the root of the tree. It
is copied to the output file, and replacements are made from
higher levels as before. This process is continued until the tree
is empty and all items have been copied to output.
   We now give a formal and generalized description of the
process.
   Let $X(1:n)$ be a file to be sorted, and let $P(1:k)$ be a complete $(m, d+1)$-tree (par. 10), where

   $$m**(d-1) < n \leq m**d.$$

   We define an (m,d)-selection sort in the following way.
Initialize the highest level of the tree with the integers 1 to
n, writing zeroes in the unused nodes at this level. A node which
contains a zero is called empty; a nonempty node points to a file
item.
   Now fill each node on the next highest level with the value
j which points to the smallest item in its filial set, and set
that son to zero to indicate that it is no longer needed on the
highest level. If all sons are zero, then set the node equal to
zero.
   Work downward, level by level, setting each node (on the
current level) to the value of that one of its sons which points
to the smallest item; replace that son by the value of that one
of its sons which points to the smallest item, and so on, until
either the highest level is reached or all sons are zero.
   When this initialization has been completed, the root of the
tree points to the smallest item in the file. Copy this item to a
working file $Z(1:n)$.
   Replace the root with the value of that one of its sons
which points to the smallest item; replace that son with the
value of that one of its sons which points to the smallest item,
and so on, until the highest level is reached. If all the sons of
a node are zero, set that node to zero.
   The root now again contains the smallest item of those that
have not yet been copied to Z. Copy it to Z.
   And so continue, until the root of the tree is zero, indicating that all items of the file have been copied to Z.
   Now copy Z back to X and the sort is complete.
   The number d is called the degree of the method. If d=1 the
method is called linear selection, and is roughly equivalent to
the method of successive minima (par. 44) carried out by surrogate. If d=2 the method is called quadratic selection; if d=3 the
method is called cubic selection, and so on.
   The number m is called the base of the method. If m=2 the
method is called binary selection; this method is also called a
tournament sort (par. 35). If m=3 the method is called ternary
selection, and so on.
   Remember that if either m or d is fixed, then the other is
automatically determined for any given file size n.

Internal Sorting
11. Sorting Methods.
    33. Selection Sorting.

Friend (1956 page 153) showed that for $n = m^{**}d$ the number
of comparisons required for an (m,d)-selection sort is approximately $(m-1)dn$, and the timing function is of the same order.
The method is therefore of timing order

n log n for fixed m,
$n^{**}(1+1/d)$ for fixed d.

The estimate $(m-1)dn$ is optimistic when n is not an even power of
m.
    The method is sequence preserving if properly programmed.

34. Replacement Selection.

A selection method is especially appealing when the internal
sort is being used as the first pass of an external sort. In this
case the object is to build up long initial strings to reduce the
number of merge passes needed.
    The items are written onto an output file as they are selec-
ted, so that a second internal copy of the segment being sorted
is not required.
    As each item is written out, a new item is read in from the
input file to take its place. If this new item is greater than or
equal than the last item written out, then it is sorted with the
others. If it is smaller than the last item written out, it is
ignored until the next string is started.
    The strings formed in this way are almost twice as long
(Gassner 1967) as the initial internal segment.

35. Tournament Sort by Surrogate.

The $(2,d)$-selection sort is shown here as a representative
of the general method. Other choices of m or d lead to programs
of comparable (but usually somewhat greater) complexity.
    This method is usually called a tournament sort, by analogy
with the selection of the winner in a tennis tournament. A complete $(2,d)$ tree vector $P(1:k)$ is used (par. 10). A subroutine
called ROOT(I) is used to replace P(I) with that one of its two
sons, say P(J), that points to the smaller item; then P(J) is
replaced in the same way, and so on until either the highest
level is reached or both sons are zero.
    This routine is called for each level d-1, d-2,..., 1 to
initialize the structure.
    Then X(P(1)) is copied to Z and ROOT(1) is called to bring
the next minimum to P(1). This sequence is repeated until all
items have been copied to Z.
    Finally, Z is copied back to X to complete the sort.
    The procedure is as follows.

```
SRT:  PROC(N); /* TOURNAMENT SORT */
      DCL P(32767) FIXED BIN(15); /* POINTER ARRAY */
```

Internal Sorting
11. Sorting Methods.
   33. Selection Sorting.
     35. Tournament Sort by Surrogate.

```
        DCL ROOT ENTRY(FIXED BIN(15));
        DCL N FIXED BIN(15);   /* FILE SIZE*/
        DCL Z(10000) FIXED BIN(15); /* FILE COPY */
        DCL LM FIXED BIN(15); /* MAXIMUM LEVEL */
        DCL (I,I1,I2) FIXED BIN(15); /* INTRALEVEL INDICES */
        DCL L FIXED BIN(15);   /* CURRENT LEVEL */
        DCL J FIXED BIN(15);   /* SELECTOR */
        DCL IZ FIXED BIN(15); /* POINTER TO Z */
        IF N<2 THEN RETURN;
        LM = 1;                /* FIND HIGHEST LEVEL */
        DO WHILE(LM<N);
          LM = 2*LM;
          END;
        DO I = 0 TO N-1;       /* INITIALIZE HIGHEST LEVEL */
          P(LM+I) = I + 1;
          END;
        DO I = N TO LM-1;
          P(LM+I) = 0;
          END;
        L = LM;                /* FILL LOWER LEVELS */
        DO WHILE(L>1);
          L = L/2;
          DO I = L TO 2*L-1;
            CALL ROOT(I);
            END;
          END;
        IZ = 1;                /* COPY TO Z */
        DO WHILE(P(1)>0);
          Z(IZ) = X(P(1));
          IZ = IZ + 1;
          CALL ROOT(1);
          END;
        DO I = 1 TO N;         /* COPY Z BACK TO X */
          X(I) = Z(I);
          END;
        RETURN;
  ROOT: PROC(I); /* FILL ROOT OF SUBTREE BASED AT I */
        DCL (I,J,I1,I2) FIXED BIN(15);
        J = I;
        DO WHILE(J<LM);
          I1 = 2*J;
          I2 = I1 + 1;
          IF P(I1)=0 THEN DO;
            IF P(I2)=0 THEN DO;
              P(J) = 0;
              J = LM;
              END;
            ELSE DO;
              P(J) = P(I2);
              P(I2) = 0;
```

Internal Sorting
11. Sorting Methods.
    33. Selection Sorting.
        35. Tournament Sort by Surrogate.


```
            J = I2;
           END;
         END;
       ELSE DO;                    /* P(I1) ¬= 0 */
         IF P(I2)=0 THEN DO;
           P(J) = P(I1);
           P(I1) = 0;
           J = I1;
           END;
         ELSE DO;
           IF X(P(I1))<=X(P(I2)) THEN DO;
             P(J) = P(I1);
             P(I1) = 0;
             J = I1;
             END;
           ELSE DO;
             P(J) = P(I2);
             P(I2) = 0;
             J = I2;
             END;
           END;
         END;
       END;
     RETURN;
     END ROOT;
     END SRT;
```

The timing results were as follows, where

N = file size
T = sorting time in milliseconds
A = $100T/(N\ LOG2(N))$
C = number of comparisons
R = number of replacements.
A superscript means multiplication by that power of 10.

N=	1	2	4	7	11	18	29	46	72	114
T=	.515	.770	1.04	1.57	2.30	3.93	5.28	9.27	16.5	23.0
A=	51.5	38.5	13.0	8.01	6.05	5.24	3.75	3.65	3.72	2.95
C=	0.00	1.00	4.67	12.6	26.8	58.4	106.	203.	386.	644.
R=	0.00	4.00	8.00	14.0	22.0	36.0	58.0	92.0	144.	228.

N=	179	280	439	686	1073	1677	2621	4096	6400	10000
T=	40.6	72.4	102.	178.	318.	451.	783.	1126	1942	3353
A=	3.03	3.18	2.64	2.76	2.94	2.51	2.63	2.29	2.40	2.52
C=	1145	2077	3336	5754	1021^1	1614^1	2737^1	4398^1	7433^1	1237^2
R=	358.	560.	878.	1372	2146	3354	5242	8192	1280^1	2000^1

The storage required is 1550 bytes plus 65,534 for the tree vector and 2n for the second copy of the file.

Internal Sorting
11. Sorting Methods.
    33. Selection Sorting.
        35. Tournament Sort by Surrogate.

    The method is sequence-preserving as written.

    ### 36. Tournament Sort, Direct.

    The tournament sort by surrogate (par. 35) requires a second
copy of the file and the additional cost of referring to the file
items indirectly. An alternative form of the procedure is given
here, in which the file items themselves, rather than their subscripts, are stored in the tree. The minimum items, as they are
determined, can then be copied back into the original vector X
rather than into a copy Z, so that the final copying from Z to X
is eliminated.
    Since, with the particular driver used, a file item can take
on the value 0, the empty nodes of the tree are marked with -1
instead.
    The procedure then looks like this.

```
SRT:   PROC(N); /* DIRECT TOURNAMENT SORT */
       DCL P(32767) FIXED BIN(15); /* POINTER ARRAY */
       DCL ROOT ENTRY(FIXED BIN(15));
       DCL N FIXED BIN(15);   /* FILE SIZE*/
       DCL LM FIXED BIN(15); /* MAXIMUM LEVEL */
       DCL (I,I1,I2) FIXED BIN(15); /* INTRALEVEL INDICES */
       DCL L FIXED BIN(15);   /* CURRENT LEVEL */
       DCL J FIXED BIN(15);   /* SELECTOR */
       IF N<2 THEN RETURN;
       LM = 1;                /* FIND HIGHEST LEVEL */
       DO WHILE(LM<N);
         LM = 2*LM;
         END;
       DO I = 0 TO N-1;       /* INITIALIZE HIGHEST LEVEL */
         P(LM+I) = X(I+1);
         END;
       DO I = N TO LM-1;
         P(LM+I) = -1;
         END;
       L = LM;                /* FILL LOWER LEVELS */
       DO WHILE(L>1);
         L = L/2;
         DO I = L TO 2*L-1;
           CALL ROOT(I);
           END;
         END;
       I = 1;                 /* COPY TO X */
       DO WHILE(P(1)>-1);
         X(I) = P(1);
         I = I + 1;
         CALL ROOT(1);
         END;
       RETURN;
```

Internal Sorting
11. Sorting Methods.
    33. Selection Sorting.
        36. Tournament Sort, Direct.


```
ROOT: PROC(I); /* FILL ROOT OF SUBTREE BASED AT I */
      DCL (I,J,I1,I2) FIXED BIN(15);
      J = I;
      DO WHILE(J<LM);
        I1 = 2*J;
        I2 = I1 + 1;
        IF P(I1)=-1 THEN DO;
          IF P(I2)=-1 THEN DO;
            P(J) = -1;
            J = LM;
            END;
          ELSE DO;
            P(J) = P(I2);
            P(I2) = -1;
            J = I2;
            END;
          END;
        ELSE DO;                    /* P(I1) ¬= -1 */
          IF P(I2)=-1 THEN DO;
            P(J) = P(I1);
            P(I1) = -1;
            J = I1;
            END;
          ELSE DO;
            IF P(I1)<=P(I2) THEN DO;
              P(J) = P(I1);
              P(I1) = -1;
              J = I1;
              END;
            ELSE DO;
              P(J) = P(I2);
              P(I2) = -1;
              J = I2;
              END;
            END;
          END;
        END;
      RETURN;
      END ROOT;
      END SRT;
```

The timing results were as follows, where

N = file size
T = sorting time in milliseconds
A = 100T/(N LOG2(N))
C = number of comparisons
R = number of replacements
A superscript means multiplication by that power of 10.

Internal Sorting
11. Sorting Methods.
  33. Selection Sorting.
    36. Tournament Sort, Direct.

N=	1	2	4	7	11	18	29	46	72	114
T=	.479	.671	.908	1.35	2.12	3.66	4.81	8.46	15.3	21.4
A=	47.9	33.6	11.3	6.86	5.56	4.88	3.41	3.33	3.45	2.75
C=	0.00	10.0	31.7	76.6	157.	319.	488.	928.	1721	2609
R=	0.00	9.00	27.0	64.0	130.	261.	382.	725.	1335	1965

N=	179	280	439	686	1073	1677	2621	4096	6400	10000
T=	38.1	66.9	92.7	163.	291.	411.	716.	1020	1759	3049
A=	2.85	2.94	2.41	2.52	2.69	2.29	2.41	2.07	2.17	2.29
C=	4699	8420	1270^1	2221^1	3899^1	5880^1	1011^2	1546^2	2635^2	4464^2
R=	3554	6343	9364	1645^1	2877^1	4267^1	7372^1	1106^2	1892^2	3228^2

The storage required is 1462 bytes plus 65,534 for the tree. The method is sequence-preserving as written.

37. Sorting in Place.

A number of methods have been described for sorting in place: the items of the file are compared two by two and interchanged if necessary, so that a second copy of the file (or equivalent surrogate) is not required. These methods are distinguished by the order in which the items are selected for the successive comparisons.

The earlier of these methods are sequence preserving and of timing order n^2. Since they are so time-consuming, they are now only of historical and pedagogical interest, since methods of order $n \log n$ are known, unless the files are very small or sequence preservation is necessary and space is not available for a sequence preserving faster method.

These slow methods are discussed briefly for the sake of completeness before going on to the faster methods. Summaries and comparisons of these methods (or some of them, at least) are given in Friend (1956), Flores (1961, 1969), and Iverson (1962). Algol programs are given in Flores (1962) and APL programs in Iverson (1962).

38. Transposition Sort.

Perhaps the most obvious internal sorting method is the transposition sort. Several passes are made over the whole file, interchanging pairs of adjacent items if they are out of order. A switch is used to determine whether an interchange actually occurred in each pass in order to terminate the process.

Bell (1958) calls this a repeated comparison sort.

We illustrate the method by the file

(4 2 7 5 3).

The item tested (against the next item to its right) in each step is underlined:

Internal Sorting
11. Sorting Methods.
    37. Sorting in Place.
        38. Transposition Sort.


```
4 2 7 5 3
2 4 7 5 3
2 4 7 5 3
2 4 5 7 3
2 4 5 3 7
2 4 5 3 7
2 4 5 3 7
2 4 3 5 7
2 4 3 5 7
2 4 3 5 7
2 3 4 5 7
2 3 4 5 7
```

The procedure looks like this.

```
SRT:  PROC(N); /* TRANSPOSITION SORT */
      DCL (I,N,Y) FIXED BIN(15);
      DCL S BIT(1) INIT('1'B); /* COMPLETION SWITCH */
      DO WHILE(S);
        S = '0'B;
        DO I = 1 TO N-1;
          IF X(I)>X(I+1) THEN DO;
            S = '1'B;
            Y = X(I);
            X(I) = X(I+1);
            X(I+1) = Y;
            END;
          END;
        END;
      END SRT;
```

The timing results were as follows, where

N = file size
T = sorting time in milliseconds
A = 100 T/(N LOG2(N))
C = number of comparisons
R = number of replacements
P = number of passes.
A superscript means multiplication by that power of 10.

N=	1	2	4	7	11	18	29	46	72	114
T=	.101	.104	.174	.296	.689	1.86	4.89	12.4	31.2	80.2
A=	10.1	5.20	2.18	1.51	1.81	2.48	3.47	4.90	7.02	10.3
C=	0.00	1.55	9.45	29.6	85.5	246.	678.	1764	4469	1170^1
R=	0.00	1.65	9.75	30.5	85.1	240.	625.	1595	3797	9678
P=	1.00	1.55	3.15	4.92	8.55	14.4	24.2	39.2	62.9	104.

52

Internal Sorting
11. Sorting Methods.
37. Sorting in Place.
38. Transposition Sort.

N=	179	280	439	686	1073
T=	198.	498.	1215	3021	7513
A=	14.8	21.9	31.5	46.7	69.5
C=	2919^1	7338^1	1801^2	4451^2	1113^3
R=	2356^1	5845^1	1428^2	3526^2	8623^2
P=	164.	263.	411.	650.	1038

The storage required is 528 bytes.
The method is sequence-preserving.
Friend (1956 p. 150) gives a formula for the expected number
of passes.

39. Alternating Transposition.

The method of alternating transposition makes successive
passes in opposite directions over the file, interchanging adjacent pairs of items if they are out of order.
Svoboda (1963) gives this as a new method.
We illustrate the method by the file

(4 2 7 5 3).

The item tested (against the next item to its right) in each step
is underlined:

```
4 2 7 5 3
2 4 7 5 3
2 4 7 5 3
2 4 5 7 3
2 4 5 3 7
2 4 5 3 7
2 4 3 5 7
2 3 4 5 7
2 3 4 5 7
```

The procedure looks like this.

```
SRT:   PROC(N);  /* ALTERNATING TRANSPOSITION */
       DCL (N,I,J) FIXED BIN(15);
       DCL S BIT(1);            /* PASS SWITCH */
SRTB:  S = '1'B;
       DO I = 1 TO N-1;
         IF X(I)>X(I+1) THEN DO;
            S = '0'B;
            Y = X(I);
            X(I) = X(I+1);
            X(I+1) = Y;
            END;
         END;
       IF S THEN RETURN;
```

Internal Sorting
11. Sorting Methods.
    37. Sorting in Place.
        39. Alternating Transposition.


```
    S = '1'B;
    DO I = N BY -1 TO 2;
      IF X(I)<X(I-1) THEN DO;
        S = '0'B;
        Y = X(I);
        X(I) = X(I-1);
        X(I-1) = Y;
        END;
      END;
    IF S THEN RETURN;
    GO TO SRTB;
    END SRT;
```

The timing results are as follows, where

N = file size
T = sorting time in milliseconds
A = 100T/(N LOG2(N))
C = number of comparisons
R = number of replacements
P = number of passes.
A superscript means multiplication by that power of 10.

N=	1	2	4	7	11	18	29	46	72	114
T=	.078	.086	.166	.296	.710	1.75	4.36	10.9	25.5	63.4
A=	7.80	4.29	2.08	1.51	1.87	2.33	3.09	4.30	5.74	8.14
C=	0.00	1.55	9.15	26.7	71.2	186.	469.	1188	2776	6865
R=	0.00	1.65	9.75	30.5	85.1	240.	625.	1595	3797	9678
P=	0.00	1.55	3.05	4.45	7.12	10.9	16.8	26.4	39.1	60.8

N=	179	280	439	686	1073
T=	154.	377.	917.	2261	5532
A=	11.5	16.5	23.8	35.0	51.2
C=	1662^1	4025^1	9768^1	2406^2	5840^2
R=	2356^1	5845^1	1428^2	3526^2	8623^2
P=	93.4	144.	223.	351.	545.

The storage required is 784 bytes.
The method is sequence-preserving.

_____
40. Odd-Even Transposition._____

   In this method each pass over the file is broken down into
two stages. In the first stage each odd-numbered item is compared
with its successor and exchanged with it if necessary. In the
second stage each even-numbered item is compared with its successor and exchanged with it if necessary.
   The passes are repeated until a pass occurs during which no
exchange takes place. The file is then in sort.
   We illustrate the method by the file

Internal Sorting
11. Sorting Methods.
    37. Sorting in Place.
       40. Odd-Even Transposition.

     (4 2 7 5 3).

The item tested (against the next item on its right) in each step
is underlined:

```
4 2 7 5 3
2 4 7 5 3
2 4 5 7 3
2 4 5 7 3
2 4 5 3 7
2 4 5 3 7
2 4 3 5 7
2 3 4 5 7
2 3 4 5 7
```

    Iverson (1962 p. 220) gives an APL program for this method.
The procedure used for the timing test looks like this.

```
SRT:    PROC(N); /* ODD-EVEN TRANSPOSITION */
        DCL (N,I,Y) FIXED BIN(15);
        DCL S BIT(1);
SRTB:   S = '1'B;
        DO I = 1 BY 2 TO N-1;
          IF X(I)>X(I+1) THEN DO;
            S = '0'B;
            Y = X(I);
            X(I) = X(I+1);
            X(I+1) = Y;
            END;
          END;
        DO I = 2 BY 2 TO N-1;
          IF X(I)>X(I+1) THEN DO;
            S = '0'B;
            Y = X(I);
            X(I) = X(I+1);
            X(I+1) = Y;
            END;
          END;
        IF S THEN RETURN;
        GO TO SRTB;
        END SRT;
```

    The timing results were as follows, where

N = file size
T = sorting time in milliseconds
A = $100T/(N \log_2(N))$
C = number of comparisons
R = number of replacements

Internal Sorting
11. Sorting Methods.
37. Sorting in Place.
40. Odd-Even Transposition.

P = number of complete passes.
A superscript means multiplication by that power of 10.

N=	1	2	4	7	11	18	29	46	72	114
T=	.075	.096	.153	.278	.512	1.28	3.10	7.71	18.7	47.5
A=	7.53	4.81	1.92	1.42	1.35	1.70	2.20	3.04	4.22	6.09
C=	0.00	1.55	8.25	23.7	57.0	151.	385.	973.	2398	6119
R=	0.00	1.65	9.75	30.5	85.1	240.	625.	1595	3797	9678
P=	1.00	1.55	2.75	3.95	5.70	8.90	13.8	21.6	32.8	54.1

N=	179	280	439	686	1073
T=	118.	288.	703.	1734	4278
A=	8.82	12.6	18.3	26.8	39.6
C=	1540^1	3767^1	9254^1	2266^2	5627^2
R=	2356^1	5845^1	1428^2	3526^2	8623^2
P=	86.5	135.	211.	331.	525.

The storage required is 672 bytes.
The method is sequence-preserving.

---

41. Bubble Sort.

This method makes several passes over the file, comparing
adjacent items and interchanging if necessary. Since each pass
bubbles the largest item to the end of the segment being sorted,
the successive passes are made over shorter and shorter segments.
If a pass does not cause an interchange then the sort is complete; it is useful to have a switch to record when this happens.
We illustrate the method by the file

(4 2 7 5 3).

The item tested (against the next item on its right) in each step
is underlined:

```
4 2 7 5 3
2 4 7 5 3
2 4 7 5 3
2 4 5 7 3
2 4 5 3 7
2 4 5 3 7
2 4 5 3 7
2 4 3 5 7
2 4 3 5 7
2 3 4 5 7
2 3 4 5 7
```

The procedure looks like this.

SRT: PROC(N); /* BUBBLE SORT */

Internal Sorting
11. Sorting Methods.
    37. Sorting in Place.
        41. Bubble Sort.

```
        DCL N FIXED BIN(15);  /* LENGTH OF FILE */
        DCL (I,J) FIXED BIN(15);
        DCL S BIT(1);          /* SWITCH */
        DCL Y FIXED BIN(15);  /* TEMPO */
        DO I = N-1 BY -1 to 1;
          S = '1'B;
          DO J = 1 to I;
            IF X(J)>X(J+1) THEN DO;
              S = '0'B;
              Y = X(J);
              X(J) = X(J+1);
              X(J+1) = Y;
              END;
            END;
          IF S THEN RETURN;
          END;
        RETURN;
        END SRT;
```

The timing results for this procedure are as follows, where

N = file size
T = sorting time in milliseconds
A = $100T/(N \ LOG2(N))$.
C = number of comparisons
R = number of replacements
P = number of passes.
A superscript means multiplication by that power of 10.

N=	1	2	4	7	11	18	29	46	72	114
T=	.088	.091	.130	.234	.504	1.24	3.05	7.72	18.3	45.7
A=	8.84	4.55	1.62	1.19	1.33	1.65	2.17	3.04	4.12	5.87
C=	0.00	1.00	5.85	19.1	51.9	146.	394.	1009	2506	6374
R=	0.00	1.65	9.75	30.5	85.1	240.	625.	1595	3797	9678
P=	0.00	1.00	2.85	4.82	8.47	14.3	24.2	39.2	62.9	104.

N=	179	280	439	686	1073
T=	113.	277.	679.	1666	4123
A=	8.42	12.2	17.6	25.8	38.2
C=	1580^1	3888^1	9569^1	2342^2	5743^2
R=	2356^1	5845^1	1428^2	3526^2	8623^2
P=	164.	263.	411.	650.	1038

The storage required for this procedure is 612 bytes.
This method is often given with passes in the opposite direction, so that items bubble toward the beginning of the file instead of toward the end.
The method is sequence preserving, of order n^2, and requires no additional storage.

Internal Sorting
11. Sorting Methods.
   37. Sorting in Place.
     41. Bubble Sort.

     Friend (1956) calls this method 'Exchanging' and gives a formula for the expected number of passes.

42. Bubble Sort without Switch.

     In the bubble sort of par. 41 we notice that the ratio of the number of passes P to the number of possible passes n-1 approaches unity as n increases. The percentage of passes saved by the switch, therefore, gets smaller as n increases. Also, the passes saved are at the end of the process, where the number of comparisons per pass is small.

     Since the switch is set in the inner loop, the question arises of whether the use of the switch saves as much time as it costs.

     To answer this question, the same procedure was tested without the use of the switch. The procedure is as follows.

```
SRT: PROC(N); /* BUBBLE WITHOUT SWITCH */
     DCL (N,I,J,Y) FIXED BIN(15);
     DO I = N-1 BY -1 TO 1;
       DO J = 1 TO I;
         IF X(J)>X(J+1) THEN DO;
           Y = X(J);
           X(J) = X(J+1);
           X(J+1) = Y;
           END;
         END;
       END;
     RETURN;
     END SRT;
```

The timing results are as follows, where

N = file size
T = sorting time in milliseconds
A = $100T/(N\ LOG2(N))$
C = number of comparisons
R = number of replacements.
A superscript means multiplication by that power of 10.

N=	1	2	4	7	11	18	29	46	72	114
T=	.073	.091	.125	.221	.520	1.28	3.15	7.76	19.1	47.8
A=	7.27	4.55	1.56	1.12	1.37	1.70	2.24	3.05	4.31	6.14
C=	0.00	1.00	6.00	21.0	55.0	153.	406.	1035	2556	6441
R=	0.00	1.65	9.75	30.5	85.1	240.	625.	1595	3797	9678
P=	0.00	1.00	3.00	6.00	10.0	17.0	28.0	45.0	71.0	113.

Internal Sorting
11. Sorting Methods.
    37. Sorting in Place.
        42. Bubble Sort without Switch.

N= 179   280   439   686   1073
T= 118.   288.   713.   1736   4254
A= 8.78   12.7   18.5   26.9   39.4
C= 1593^1 3906^1 9614^1 2350^2 5751^2
R= 2356^1 5845^1 1428^2 3526^2 8623^2
P= 178.   279.   438.   687.   1072

The storage required is 540 bytes.
The method is sequence-preserving.
Over the range tested, the switch does save a little time.

----
43. Funnel Sort.

Just as the bubble sort (par. 41) derives from transposition
(par. 38) by taking advantage of the fact that each pass moves at
least one item to its final location, the funnel sort derives
from alternating transposition (par. 39).

Successive passes are made in opposite directions, and each
pass is one item shorter than the preceding one. A switch S
terminates the process as soon as a pass causes no exchanges.

We illustrate the method by the file

    (4 2 7 5 3)

The item tested (against the item on its right) in each step is
underlined:

    4 2 7 5 3
    2 4 7 5 3
    2 4 7 5 3
    2 4 5 7 3
    2 4 5 3 7
    2 4 3 5 7
    2 3 4 5 7
    2 3 4 5 7
    2 3 4 5 7

The procedure looks like this.

```
SRT:  PROC(N); /* FUNNEL SORT */
      DCL (N,I,J,Y) FIXED BIN(15);
      DCL S BIT(1);
      DO I = 1 TO N/2;
        S = '1'B;
        DO J = I TO N-I;
          IF X(J)>X(J+1) THEN DO;
            S = '0'B;
            Y = X(J);
            X(J) = X(J+1);
            X(J+1) = Y;
```

59

Internal Sorting
11. Sorting Methods.
   37. Sorting in Place.
      43. Funnel Sort.

```
          END;
        END;
      IF S THEN RETURN;
      S = '1'B;
      DO J = N-I BY -1 TO I+1;
        IF X(J)<X(J-1) THEN DO;
          S = '0'B;
          Y = X(J);
          X(J) = X(J-1);
          X(J-1) = Y;
          END;
        END;
      IF S THEN RETURN;
      END;
    RETURN;
    END SRT;
```

The timing results are as follows, where

```
N = file size
T = sorting time in milliseconds
A = 100T/(N LOG2(N))
C = number of comparisons
R = number of replacements
P = number of passes.
```
A superscript means multiplication by that power of 10.

N=	1	2	4	7	11	18	29	46	72	114
T=	.073	.099	.153	.252	.483	1.14	2.72	6.84	16.1	39.9
A=	7.28	4.94	1.92	1.28	1.27	1.52	1.93	2.69	3.61	5.12
C=	0.00	1.00	5.85	18.2	48.7	130.	334.	849.	2026	5038
R=	0.00	1.65	9.75	30.5	85.1	240.	625.	1595	3797	9678
P=	0.00	1.55	3.05	4.38	7.12	10.9	16.8	26.4	39.1	60.8

N=	179	280	439	686	1073
T=	97.1	236.	575.	1428	3520
A=	7.24	10.3	14.9	22.1	32.6
C=	1229^1	2989^1	7288^1	1790^2	4358^2
R=	2356^1	5845^1	1428^2	3526^2	8623^2
P=	93.4	144.	223.	351.	545.

The storage required is 816 bytes.
The method is sequence-preserving.

----
44. Successive Minima.

In this method we interchange X(1) with the minimal item in
the whole file, X(2) with the minimal item of the remaining n-1,
and so on. The procedure looks like this.

Internal Sorting
11. Sorting Methods.
    37. Sorting in Place.
        44. Successive Minima.


```
SRT:    PROC(N); /* SUCCESSIVE MINIMA */
        DCL (N,I,J,K,Y) FIXED BIN(15);
        DO I = 1 TO N-1;
          K = I;
          DO J = I+1 TO N;
            IF X(J)<X(K) THEN K = J;
            END;
          IF K>I THEN DO;
            Y = X(I);
            X(I) = X(K);
            X(K) = Y;
            END;
          END;
        RETURN;
        END SRT;
```

The method is sequence-preserving and of order n^2.

This method is useful in the first pass of an external sort, as described in par. 34. It corresponds functionally to linear selection (par. 33).

The timing results were as follows, where

N = file size
T = sorting time in milliseconds
A = $100T/(N \text{ LOG2}(N))$
C = number of comparisons
R = number of replacements.
A superscript means multiplication by that power of 10.

N=	1	2	4	7	11	18	29	46	72	114
T=	.068	.088	.143	.239	.455	.978	2.23	5.20	12.1	29.4
A=	6.76	4.42	1.79	1.22	1.20	1.30	1.58	2.05	2.72	3.77
C=	0.00	1.00	6.00	21.0	55.0	153.	405.	1036	2556	6441
R=	0.00	1.65	6.30	12.8	23.5	42.7	74.1	126.	200.	326.

N=	179	280	439	686	1073
T=	71.1	173.	449.	1050	2561
A=	5.31	7.60	11.6	16.2	23.7
C=	1593^1	3906^1	96141^1	23502^2	57512^2
R=	520.	821.	1298	2035	3195

The amount of storage required was 572 bytes.

---

45. Ranking Sort.

The ranking sort is equivalent to an M-sift (par. 50) with M=1. Each item in turn is sifted down to its proper place among the items that originally preceded it in the file. Friend (1956) calls this method 'Inserting'. Bell (1958) calls it an insertion sort.

Internal Sorting
11. Sorting Methods.
   37. Sorting in Place.
      45. Ranking Sort.

Sander-Cederlof (1970) calls this a sawtooth sort.
We illustrate the method by the file

(4 2 7 5 3).

The item tested (against the item on its right) in each step is
underlined:

```
4 2 7 5 3
2 4 7 5 3
2 4 7 5 3
2 4 5 7 3
2 4 5 7 3
2 4 5 3 7
2 4 3 5 7
2 3 4 5 7
2 3 4 5 7
```

The procedure looks like this.

```
SRT:   PROC(N); /* RANKING SORT */
       DCL (N,Y,I,J) FIXED BIN(15);
       DO J = 1 to N-1;
         Y = X(J+1);
         DO I = J BY -1 TO 1 WHILE(Y<X(I));
           X(I+1) = X(I);
           END;
         X(I+1) = Y;
         END;
       RETURN;
       END SRT;
```

The timing results for this procedure are as follows, where

N = file size
T = sorting time in milliseconds
A = 100T/(N LOG2(N))
C = number of comparisons
R = number of replacements.
A superscript means multiplication by that power of 10.

N=	1	2	4	7	11	18	29	46	72	114
T=	.081	.081	.120	.195	.361	.822	1.83	4.29	9.79	24.1
A=	8.06	4.03	1.49	.992	.950	1.10	1.30	1.69	2.20	3.10
C=	0.00	1.55	6.25	16.2	38.4	96.9	236.	577.	1337	3339
R=	0.00	2.55	9.25	22.2	48.4	114.	264.	622.	1408	3452

Internal Sorting
11. Sorting Methods.
   37. Sorting in Place.
      45. Ranking Sort.

N=	179	280	439	686	1073
T=	58.3	142.	343.	841.	2060
A=	4.35	6.22	8.90	13.0	19.1
C=	8030	1976^1	4804^1	1182^2	2885^2
R=	8208	2004^1	4847^1	1189^2	2896^2

The storage required for this procedure is 563 bytes.

The method is sequence-preserving, of order n^2, and requires no additional storage. It is somewhat faster than the bubble sort.

Wierzbowski (1965) describes an insertion sort using a doubly-linked list with a separate directory to segments thereof to save scanning time.

46. Binary Ranking Sort.

You will notice that for any value of J (in the outer loop), the first J items of the file are already in order, so that the correct position for the (J+1)-st item can be found by binary search. If this is done, the number of comparisons required becomes of order $n \log n$, but the number of replacements remains the same as before.

The program then looks like this:

```
SRT:   PROC(N); /* BINARY RANKING SORT */
       DCL (N,Y,I,J,IL,IU) FIXED BIN(15);
       DO J = 1 TO N-1;
         Y = X(J+1);
         IL = 0;
         IU = J+1;
         DO WHILE(IU-IL>1);
           I = (IL+IU)/2;
           IF Y<X(I) THEN IU = I;
                     ELSE IL = I;
           END;
         DO I = J BY -1 TO IU;
           X(I+1) = X(I);
           END;
         X(I+1) = Y;
         END;
       RETURN;
       END SRT;
```

The timing results are as follows, where

```
N = file size
T = sorting time in milliseconds
A = 100T/(N LOG2(N))
C = number of comparisons
R = number of replacements.
```

Internal Sorting
11. Sorting Methods.
   37. Sorting in Place.
      46. Binary Ranking Sort.

A superscript means multiplication by that power of 10.

N=	1	2	4	7	11	18	29	46	72	114
T=	.078	.096	.185	.322	.588	1.14	2.22	4.45	3.66	18.3
A=	7.80	4.81	2.31	1.64	1.54	1.52	1.57	1.75	1.95	2.35
C=	0.00	1.00	4.60	12.7	25.9	53.1	104.	194.	349.	626.
R=	0.00	2.55	9.25	22.2	48.4	114.	264.	622.	1408	3452

N=	179	280	439	686	1073
T=	37.5	81.3	181.	412.	954.
A=	2.80	3.57	4.69	6.38	8.83
C=	1096	1893	3254	5515	9319
R=	8208	2004^1	4847^1	1189^2	2896^2

The storage required for this version of the procedure is 652 bytes.

---

47. P-Operator Method.

Bose and Nelson (Bose 1962) describe a method of sorting based on finding the shortest sequence of comparisons and possible exchanges of pairs of items.

Given a file $X(1:n)$ to be sorted and two integers $1 \leq i < j \leq n$, define the simple P-operator $P(i,j)$ as a comparison of $KX(i)$ and $KX(j)$, followed by an exchange of the items $X(i)$ and $X(j)$ if $KX(i) > KX(j)$.

In what follows, it will be convenient to denote the simple operator $P(i,j)$ by the ordered triple $(1,i,j)$.

For any two sequences

$$i, \ i+1, \ i+2, \ \ldots, \ i+x-1$$
$$j, \ j+1, \ j+2, \ \ldots, \ j+y-1$$

of consecutive integers such that

$$1 \leq i \leq i+x-1 < j \leq j+y-1 \leq n$$

Bose and Nelson define a complex P-operator

$$P[\ (i,i+1,\ldots,i+x-1),(j,j+1,\ldots,j+y-1) \ ]$$

in a way to be described shortly. It is convenient for our purposes to denote this complex operator by the ordered quintuple $(3,i,x,j,y)$. The definition of the complex operator in terms of simple ones is by recursion on x and y:

$$(3,i,0,j,y) = 1 \text{ (the null operator)}$$
$$(3,i,x,j,0) = 1$$

(The symbols with x or $y = 0$ do not actually occur in the al-

Internal Sorting
11. Sorting Methods.
    47. P-Operator Method.

gorithm, but are included for the sake of logical completeness.)

        (3,i,1,j,1) = (1,i,j)
        (3,i,1,j,2) = (1,i,j+1)(1,i,j)
        (3,i,2,j,1) = (1,i,j)(1,i+1,j)

where a product of operators indicates that they are to be carried out in order, starting at the left.
    To extend the definition to the case where x and y are both greater than 1, we introduce the integer variables a and b:

    b = [(y+1)/2] if x is even
      = [y/2]   if x is odd
    a = [x/2].

and we can then define

$$(3,i,x,j,y)=(3,i,a,j,b)(3,i+a,x-a,j+b,y-b)(3,i+a,x-a,j,b)$$

You will easily verify that if x>1 then both a and x-a are less than x; if y>1 then both b and y-b are less than y, so the recursive definition is complete.
    They define one final type of operator on single sequences of consecutive integers, namely P*(i,i+1,...,i+x-1), which we denote by the ordered triple (2,i,x), also by recursion on x:

    (2,i,1) = 1, the null operator.

For x>1 define the integer variable a by a = [x/2], and then

    (2,i,x)=(2,i,a)(2,i+a,x-a)(3,i,a,i+a,x-a).

You will easily verify that this definition is also complete. Of course the conditions

    1 ≤ i ≤ i+x-1 ≤ n

are assumed to hold.
    The sorting procedure now consists of the following operations on a sequence S of these operators.
    Initially set S = (2,1,n).
    If S is not empty, perform its leftmost operation. That is, if the first n-tuple is (1,i,j) then compare X(i) and X(j) and exchange them if necessary. Otherwise replace the n-tuple according to its definition. So continue until S is empty.
    The inductive proof (on decreasing x's and y's) that the process terminates is straightforward. The fact that when the process terminates the file is in sort is Theorem 7 of the cited paper.
    The method is not sequence-preserving.
    We illustrate the method for n=5, computing the single

Internal Sorting
11. Sorting Methods.
    47. P-Operator Method.

interchanges (1,i,j) first, and then carrying them out. At each
step we underline the symbol to be replaced.

S
(2,1,5)
(2,1,2) (2,3,3) (3,1,2,3,3)
(2,1,1) (2,2,1) (3,1,1,2,1) (2,3,3) (3,1,2,3,3)
(2,2,1) (3,1,1,2,1) (2,3,3) (3,1,2,3,3)
(3,1,1,2,1) (2,3,3) (3,1,2,3,3)
(1,1,2) (2,3,3) (3,1,2,3,3)
(1,1,2) (2,3,1) (2,4,2) (3,3,1,4,2) (3,1,2,3,3)
(1,1,2) (2,4,2) (3,3,1,4,2) (3,1,2,3,3)
(1,1,2) (2,4,1) (2,5,1) (3,4,1,5,1) (3,3,1,4,2) (3,1,2,3,3)
(1,1,2) (2,5,1) (3,4,1,5,1) (3,3,1,4,2) (3,1,2,3,3)
(1,1,2) (3,4,1,5,1) (3,3,1,4,2) (3,1,2,3,3)
(1,1,2) (1,4,5) (3,3,1,4,2) (3,1,2,3,3)
(1,1,2) (1,4,5) (1,3,5) (1,3,4) (3,1,2,3,3)
(1,1,2) (1,4,5) (1,3,5) (1,3,4) (3,1,1,3,2) (3,2,1,5,1) (3,2,1,3,2)
(1,1,2) (1,4,5) (1,3,5) (1,3,4) (1,1,4) (1,1,3) (3,2,1,5,1) (3,2,1,3,2)
(1,1,2) (1,4,5) (1,3,5) (1,3,4) (1,1,4) (1,1,3) (1,2,5) (3,2,1,3,2)
(1,1,2) (1,4,5) (1,3,5) (1,3,4) (1,1,4) (1,1,3) (1,2,5) (1,2,4) (1,2,3)

    We are now in a position to carry out the indicated sequence
of test-interchanges on a file of five items, say

    (4 2 7 5 3).

At each step we underline the two items which are to be compared
and then interchanged if necessary:

    4 2 7 5 3
    2 4 7 5 3
    2 4 7 3 5
    2 4 5 3 7
    2 4 3 5 7
    2 4 3 5 7
    2 4 3 5 7
    2 4 3 5 7
    2 4 3 5 7
    2 3 4 5 7

And we see that the file does in fact end up in sort.

----
    48. Direct Procedure.

    A computer procedure to carry out this process requires a
pushdown list for the n-tuples in the string S. The maximum number g(n) of numbers in this pushdown list clearly depends on n.
Experiment indicates that for n>3 we have g(n) < 10 LOG2(n).
    The test procedure is as follows.

Internal Sorting
11. Sorting Methods.
    47. P-Operator Method.
       48. Direct Procedure.


```
SRT:    PROC(N); /* BOSE-NELSON SORT */
        DCL N FIXED BIN(15);    /* FILE SIZE */
        DCL V(150) FIXED BIN(15); /* PUSHDOWN LIST */
        DCL P FIXED BIN(15);   /* PUSHDOWN POINTER */
        DCL L(3) LABEL(L1,L2,L3) INIT(L1,L2,L3);
        DCL (I1,I2,M1,M2,M3,M4,M,Y) FIXED BIN(15);
        V(1) = N;              /* INITIALIZE PUSHDOWN */
        V(2) = 1;
        V(3) = 2;
        P = 3;
SRTB:   IF P<1 THEN RETURN;    /* TAKE NEXT TERM */
        GO TO L(V(P));
L1:     /* SIMPLE INTERCHANGE TEST */
        I1 = V(P-1);              /* FIRST SUBSCRIPT */
        I2 = V(P-2);              /* SECOND SUBSCRIPT */
        P = P - 3;
        IF X(I1)>X(I2) THEN DO; /* MAKE COMPARISON */
           Y = X(I1);
           X(I1) = X(I2);
           X(I2) = Y;
           END;
        GO TO SRTB;
L2:     /* DO A P* TRIPLE */
        I1 = V(P-1);            /* FIRST SUBSCRIPT */
        M1 = V(P-2);            /* LENGTH OF SEGMENT */
        P = P - 3;
        IF M1<2 THEN GO TO SRTB;
        M = M1/2;
        V(P+5) = 3;
        V(P+8), V(P+11) = 2;
        V(P+1), V(P+6) = M1 - M;
        V(P+2), V(P+7) = I1 + M;
        V(P+3), V(P+9) = M;
        V(P+4), V(P+10) = I1;
        P = P + 11;
        GO TO SRTB;
L3:     /* DO A P QUINTUPLE */
        I1 = V(P-1);              /* FIRST SUBSCRIPT */
        M1 = V(P-2);              /* FIRST LENGTH */
        I2 = V(P-3);              /* SECOND SUBSCRIPT */
        M2 = V(P-4);              /* SECOND LENGTH */
        P = P - 5;
        IF M1+M2<4 THEN DO;     /* TEST SMALL SEGMENTS */
           IF M1=1 THEN DO;
              IF M2=1 THEN DO;
                 V(P+1) = I2;

                 V(P+2) = I1;
                 V(P+3) = 1;
                 P = P + 3;
```

Internal Sorting
11. Sorting Methods.
    47. P-Operator Method.
       48. Direct Procedure.

```
             GO TO SRTB;
             END;
           ELSE DO;
             V(P+1) = I2;
             V(P+2), V(P+5) = I1;
             V(P+3), V(P+6) = 1;
             V(P+4) = I2 + 1;
             P = P + 6;
             GO TO SRTB;
             END;
           END;
         ELSE DO;
           V(P+1), V(P+4) = I2;
           V(P+2) = I1 + 1;
           V(P+3), V(P+6) = 1;
           V(P+5) = I1;
           P = P + 6;
           GO TO SRTB;
           END;
         END;
       IF MOD(M1,2)=0 THEN M4 = (M2+1)/2; /* DO LARGE SEGMENTS */
                       ELSE M4 = M2/2;
       M3 = M1/2;
       V(P+1), V(P+11) = M4;
       V(P+2), V(P+12) = I2;
       V(P+3), V(P+8) = M1 - M3;
       V(P+4), V(P+9) = I1 + M3;
       V(P+5), V(P+10), V(P+15) = 3;
       V(P+6) = M2 - M4;
       V(P+7) = I2 + M4;
       V(P+13) = M3;
       V(P+14) = I1;
       P = P + 15;
       GO TO SRTB;
       END SRT;
```

The timing results are as follows, where

N = file size
T = sorting time in milliseconds
A = $100T/(N \log_2(N))$
C = number of comparisons
R = number of replacements.
A superscript means multiplication by that power of 10.

N=	1	2	4	7	11	18	29	46	72	114
T=	.174	.211	.474	1.04	1.92	4.41	10.2	19.8	41.8	92.1
A=	17.4	10.5	5.92	5.28	5.04	5.88	7.24	7.80	9.42	11.8
C=	0.00	1.00	5.00	16.0	38.0	90.0	191.	422.	900.	1824
R=	0.00	1.65	8.55	25.3	64.0	163.	324.	662.	1344	2582

Internal Sorting
11. Sorting Methods.
    47. P-Operator Method.
       48. Direct Procedure.

N=	179	280	439	686	1073
T=	178.	375.	809.	1540	3326
A=	13.3	16.5	21.0	23.8	30.8
C=	3924	8171	1610[1]	3425[1]	6912[1]
R=	4897	9375	1595[1]	3055[1]	5584[1]

The storage required is 2638 bytes, including 300 bytes for the pushdown list.

49. Hibbard's Modification.

Hibbard (1963b) gives an interesting method of selecting, in succession, the pairs of items to be compared. The procedure below is a free translation of his Algol program. The problem is to select the sequence of pairs (i,j) of integers such that the corresponding sequence of comparisons $P(i,j)$ will carry out the sort.

For this purpose, $i-1$ and $j-1$ are expressed in binary, using the two BIT vectors BX and BY, and the individual bits are then manipulated in such a way as to generate the correct sequence. Special tests are required to cover the case where n is not a power of two.

The procedure is as follows.

```
SRT:    PROC(N);  /* BOSE-HIBBARD */
        DCL (I1,I2,J,L,N,Y) FIXED BIN(15);
        DCL (BX(0:15),BY(0:15)) BIT(1);
        DCL SUM ENTRY((*)BIT(1)) RETURNS(FIXED BIN(15));
        J = 2;                   /* L = LOG2(N) */
        DO L = 1 TO N;
          IF J>N THEN GO TO E;
          J = J + J;
          END;
E:      L = L - 1;
        BX, BY = '0'B;           /* INITIALIZE BIT VECTORS */
        BY(0) = '1'B;
A:      I1 = SUM(BX);            /* MAKE COMPARISON */
        I2 = SUM(BY);
        IF X(I1)>X(I2) THEN DO;
          Y = X(I1);
          X(I1) = X(I2);
          X(I2) = Y;
          END; ELSE;
        J = 0;
C:      IF BX(J) THEN DO;
          IF BY(J) THEN DO;
            BY(J) = '0'B;
            GO TO A;
            END;
```

Internal Sorting
11. Sorting Methods.
    47. P-Operator Method.
        49. Hibbard's Modification.

```
          ELSE DO;
            BX(J) = '0'B;
            J = J + 1;
            GO TO C;
            END;
          END;
        ELSE DO;
          IF BY(J) THEN DO;
FIRST:      BX(J), BY(J) = '0'B;
            IF J = L THEN RETURN;
            ELSE DO;
              J = J + 1;
              IF BY(J) THEN DO;
D:              BX(J) = '0'B;
                BY(J) = '1'B;
                GO TO A;
                END;
              ELSE DO;
                BX(J), BY(J) = '1'B;
                I2 = SUM(BY);
                IF I2>N THEN GO TO FIRST; ELSE;
                IF I2<N THEN J = 0; ELSE;
                GO TO D;
                END;
              END;
            END;
          ELSE DO;
            BX(J), BY(J) = '1'B;
            IF SUM(BY)<=N THEN GO TO A;
            ELSE DO;
              BY(J) = '0'B;
              GO TO A;
              END;
            END;
          END;
SUM:  PROC(B) RETURNS(FIXED BIN(15)); /* COMPUTE INDEX */
      DCL B(*) BIT(1);
      DCL (S,P) FIXED BIN(15) INIT(1);
      DCL J FIXED BIN(15);
      DO J = 0 TO L;
        IF B(J) THEN S = S + P;
        P = 2*P;
        END;
      RETURN(S);
      END SUM;
      END SRT;
```

The timing results are as follows, where

N = file size

Internal Sorting
11. Sorting Methods.
    47. P-Operator Method.
       49. Hibbard's Modification.

T = sorting time in milliseconds
A = $100T/(N \, LOG2(N))$
C = number of comparisons
R = number of replacements.
A superscript means multiplication by that power of 10.

N=	1	2	4	7	11	18	29	46	72	114
T=	1.09	1.40	3.10	7.89	19.6	50.4	104.	251.	583.	1171
A=	109.	70.0	38.8	40.1	51.6	67.1	73.8	98.9	131.	150.
C=	0.00	1.00	5.00	16.0	38.0	90.0	191.	422.	900.	1824
R=	0.00	1.57	7.65	26.9	58.0	144.	293.	611.	1244	2189

N=	179	280
T=	2728	6044
A=	204.	266.
C=	3924	8171
R=	4219	8258

    The storage required is 2476 bytes.
    The slowness of this procedure, as compared with the one given in par. 48, is partly inherent in the method and partly a result of the high cost of bit-picking in PL/1.

50. Sifting: the Shell Sort.

    For any integer M ($1 \leq M \leq n$) we define an M-sift of the file X(1:n) as follows:

```
      DO J = 1 TO N-M;
        Y = X(J+M);
        DO I = J BY -M TO 1;
          IF Y>=X(I) THEN GO TO OUT;
          X(I+M) = X(I);
          END;
 OUT:    X(I) = Y;
        END;
```

    What happens, as the coding shows, is that the N items of the file are separated (conceptually) into M equivalence classes modulo M with respect to their subscripts. The members of each class may be thought of as standing on the rungs of a ladder, with M-1 items from other classes between each pair of rungs. Each item in turn climbs down its ladder (trading rungs successively with the next lower members of its class) until it takes its correct position among the previously sorted members of its class.
    Another way of putting it is that a ranking sort (par. 45) is done within each group.
    The complete sort carries out successive M-sifts with smaller and smaller values of M until a final sift with M=1 completes

the sort. Variations of this method are distinguished by the procedure used for determining the sequence of M's.
   The fact that such a sequence of M-sifts does result in an efficient complete sort follows from the proof by Gale and Karp (1970) that one M-sift does not disrupt a preceding one.

51. Original Shell Sort.

   Shell (1960), the originator of the method, took [N/2] as the first value of M and used the formula

   M = [M/2]

thereafter.
   We illustrate the procedure with the file

   (4 2 7 5 8 1 3)

The two items which are compared at each step (and interchanged if necessary) are underlined. For a file of 7 items we start out with M=3:

```
4 2 7 5 8 1 3
4 2 7 5 8 1 3
4 2 7 5 8 1 3
4 2 1 5 8 7 3
4 2 1 3 8 7 5
3 2 1 4 8 7 5
```

We now take M=1:

```
3 2 1 4 8 7 5
2 3 1 4 8 7 5
2 1 3 4 8 7 5
1 2 3 4 8 7 5
1 2 3 4 8 7 5
1 2 3 4 8 7 5
1 2 3 4 7 8 5
1 2 3 4 7 8 5
1 2 3 4 7 5 8
1 2 3 4 5 7 8
1 2 3 4 5 7 8.
```

   The procedure looks like this.

```
SRT:   PROC(N); /* SHELL SORT */
       DCL (N,M,Y,I,J) FIXED BIN(15);
       IF N<2 THEN RETURN;
       M = N;
SRTF:  M = M/2;
       DO J = 1 TO N-M;
```

Internal Sorting
11. Sorting Methods.
    50. Sifting: the Shell Sort.
        51. Original Shell Sort.

```
          Y = X(J+M);
          DO I = J BY -M TO 1;
            IF X(I)<Y THEN GO TO SRTH;
            X(I+M) = X(I);
            END;
  SRTH:    X(I+M) = Y;
          END;
       IF M>1 THEN GO TO SRTF;
       RETURN;
       END SRT;
```

The timing results were as follows, where

N = file size
T = sorting time in milliseconds
A = 100T/(N LOG2(N))
C = number of comparisons
R = number of replacements.
A superscript means multiplication by that power of 10.

N=	1	2	4	7	11	18	29	46	72	114
T=	.070	.099	.177	.286	.572	1.12	1.89	3.72	7.10	12.2
A=	7.02	4.94	2.21	1.45	1.50	1.49	1.34	1.46	1.60	1.56
C=	0.00	1.00	6.02	14.7	35.0	78.7	141.	282.	555.	973.
R=	0.00	2.57	12.7	26.9	65.3	143.	246.	494.	955.	1612

N=	179	280	439	686	1073	1677	2621
T=	22.2	40.4	65.8	116.	215.	355.	620.
A=	1.66	1.77	1.71	1.80	1.99	1.98	2.08
C=	1790	3292	5455	9697	1823^1	3042^1	5298^1
R=	2963	5399	8777	1557^1	2843^1	4640^1	8062^1

The storage required is 692 bytes.
The method is not sequence-preserving.

52. Frank and Lazarus Modification.

Frank and Lazarus (1960) analyzed the process and found a timing function of order $n(\log n)^2$. They noticed that when the binary expression for n contains a large number of zeros, the groups tend to remain coherent during successive sifts, instead of mixing properly.

They therefore ensure that successive divisors are odd, and also divide by approximately 4 instead of 2 for large M. The procedure looks like this.

```
  SRT:   PROC(N); /* SHELL-FRANK SORT */
         DCL (N,M,Y,I,J) FIXED BIN(15);
         IF N<2 THEN RETURN;
         M = N;
```

Internal Sorting
11. Sorting Methods.
    50. Sifting: the Shell Sort.
        52. Frank and Lazarus Modification.


```
  SRTF: IF M>15 THEN I = 8;
                ELSE I = 4;
        J = M/I;
        M = 2*J + 1;
        DO J = 1 TO N-M;
          Y = X(J+M);
          DO I = J BY -M TO 1;
            IF X(I)<Y THEN GO TO SRTH;
            X(I+M) = X(I);
            END;
  SRTH:   X(I+M) = Y;
          END;
        IF M>1 THEN GO TO SRTF;
        RETURN;
        END SRT;
```

The timing results were as follows, where

```
N = file size
T = sorting time in milliseconds
A = 100T/(N LOG2(N))
C = number of comparisons
R = number of replacements.
```
A superscript means multiplication by that power of 10.

N=	1	2	4	7	11	18	29	46	72	114
T=	.068	.109	.174	.325	.604	1.11	1.96	3.82	6.71	11.4
A=	6.75	5.46	2.18	1.65	1.59	1.48	1.39	1.51	1.51	1.47
C=	0.00	1.00	5.30	14.7	33.4	70.0	135.	275.	494.	881.
R=	0.00	2.57	10.5	26.9	62.7	122.	221.	457.	782.	1340

N=	179	280	439	686	1073	1677	2621
T=	22.1	37.5	64.3	116.	198.	316.	551.
A=	1.65	1.65	1.67	1.80	1.83	1.76	1.85
C=	1662	2909	5043	8993	1576[1]	2591[1]	4528[1]
R=	2559	4318	7255	1313[1]	2224[1]	3603[1]	6372[1]

The storage required is 744 bytes.
The method is not sequence-preserving.

---

53. Hibbard's Modification.

Hibbard (1963) ensured incoherence by taking the first M as
one less than a power of two and using the simple formula M =
[M/2] thereafter. Each of the M's is then one less than a power
of two, and therefore odd.
    The procedure looks like this.

```
  SRT:  PROC(N); /* SHELL-HIBBARD SORT */
        DCL (N,M,Y,I,J) FIXED BIN(15);
```

Internal Sorting
11. Sorting Methods.
50. Sifting: the Shell Sort.
53. Hibbard's Modification.

```
        IF N<2 THEN RETURN;
        M = 4;                        /* CHOOSE FIRST DIVISOR */
        DO I = 1 TO N WHILE(M<N);
          M = M + M;
          END;
        M = M - 1;
 SRTF:  M = M/2;
        DO J = 1 TO N-M;
          Y = X(J+M);
          DO I = J BY -M TO 1;
            IF X(I)<Y THEN GO TO SRTH;
            X(I+M) = X(I);
            END;
 SRTH:    X(I+M) = Y;
          END;
        IF M>1 THEN GO TO SRTF;
        RETURN;
        END SRT;
```

The timing results were as follows, where

```
N = file size
T = sorting time in milliseconds
A = 100T/(N LOG2(N))
C = number of comparisons
R = number of replacements.
```
A superscript means multiplication by that power of 10.

N=	1	2	4	7	11	18	29	46	72	114
T=	.081	.109	.156	.307	.590	1.12	2.09	4.00	7.17	13.1
A=	8.06	5.46	1.95	1.56	1.55	1.50	1.48	1.58	1.61	1.68
C=	0.00	1.00	5.12	14.7	31.4	68.1	137.	270.	503.	924.
R=	0.00	2.57	9.27	26.9	58.3	121.	241.	465.	852.	1547

N=	179	280	439	686	1073	1677	2621
T=	23.2	41.2	71.9	125.	214.	366.	633.
A=	1.73	1.81	1.87	1.93	1.98	2.04	2.13
C=	1665	2989	5279	9230	1607^1	2779^1	4855^1
R=	2761	4876	8522	1474^1	2535^1	4341^1	7466^1

The storage required is 788 bytes.
The method is not sequence-preserving.

54. Assembly Language Comparison.

Although the cost in computer time of using a high level language such as PL/1 is not the main subject of this investigation, one comparison with assembly language may be instructive. The same version of the Shell sort was therefore written in PL/1 and in 360 assembly language.

Internal Sorting
11. Sorting Methods.
    50. Sifting: the Shell Sort.
        54. Assembly Language Comparison.

    The PL/1 version is as follows.

```
 SRT:    PROC(N); /* SHELL SORT */
         DCL (N,M,Y,I,J) FIXED BIN(15);
         M = N;
 SRTF:   M = MAX(1,M/3.141592);
         DO J = 1 TO N-M;
           Y = X(J+M);
           DO I = J BY -M TO 1;
             IF X(I)<Y THEN GO TO SRTH;
             X(I+M) = X(I);
             END;
 SRTH:    X(I+M) = Y;
           END;
         IF M>1 THEN GO TO SRTF;
         RETURN;
         END SRT;
```

    The timing results for this procedure are as follows, where

    N = file size
    T = sorting time in milliseconds
    A = $100T/(N \log_2(N))$
    C = number of comparisons
    R = number of replacements.
    A superscript means multiplication by that power of 10.

N=	1	2	4	7	11	18	29	46	72	114
T=	.078	.096	.135	.231	.462	.918	2.03	4.86	6.34	15.3
A=	7.80	4.81	1.69	1.18	1.22	1.22	1.44	1.91	1.43	1.96
C=	0.00	1.00	5.12	14.5	38.6	92.6	228.	567.	694.	1740
R=	0.00	2.15	7.42	17.6	43.0	97.0	233.	573.	739.	1809

N=	179	280	439	686	1073	1677	2621
T=	34.3	45.1	111.	165.	316.	669.	1165
A=	2.56	1.98	2.87	2.56	2.93	3.73	3.91
C=	4013	5124	1306^1	1914^1	3713^1	7959^1	1369^2
R=	4116	5322	1338^1	1967^1	3797^1	8092^1	1390^2

    The storage required for this procedure is 688 bytes.
    The assembly language version, coded by Mr. Alexander B. Murphy, is as follows.

```
SRT       CSECT
          SAVE   (14,12),,*
          USING  SRT,15
*     NOTE:  $ BEFORE A VARIABLE DENOTES 2 TIMES THE
*            CORRESPONDING PL1 VARIABLE
          L      3,0(1)  3=.N
          LH     0,0(3)  0=N
```

Internal Sorting
11. Sorting Methods.
    50. Sifting: the Shell Sort.
        54. Assembly Language Comparison.

```
            SLL     0,1 0=$N
            LR      6,0 6=OFFSET TO LAST ELEMENT=$M
            L       1,4(1) 1=.ADV
            L       1,0(1) 1=.VIRTUAL ORIGIN=X(1) -2
            SR      11,11   CLEAR 11 SET UP FOR BXH
            LA      4,2 4= CONSTANT 2
SRTF        SR      7,7 CLEAR 7
            SRDL    6,15 SET UP FOR DIVSION $M*2**17
            D       6,PI       PI= PI*2**17
            CR      7,4 COMPARE QUOTIENT WITH 2
            BNL     OK
            LR      7,4 SET 7 TO 2
OK          LR      6,7
            N       6,=X'FFFFFFFE' 6 CONTAINS NEW $M
            LCR     10,6 10 =-$M
            LR      8,4 LOAD 8 WITH 2   8=$J
            LR      5,0 LOAD 5 WITH $N
            SR      5,6 5=$N-$M
OUTER       LR      2,8
            AR      2,6 2=$J+$M
            LH      7,0(1,2)   7=X($J+$M)=Y
            LR      9,8 LOAD 9 WITH 8   $I=$J
INNER       LH      12,0(1,9) LOAD 12 WITH X($I)
            CR      12,7  X($I) : Y
            BL      SRTH BRANCH IFF X($I)<Y  I.E.   12<7
            LR      14,9
            AR      14,6   14=$I+$M
            STH     12,0(1,14)
            BXH     9,10,INNER
SRTH        LR      14,9
            AR      14,6   14=$I+$M
            STH     7,0(1,14)   X($I+$M)=Y
            BXLE    8,4,OUTER
            CR      6,4
            BH      SRTF
            RETURN  (14,12)
PI          DC      XL4'0006487F'   =3.14590 X 2**17
            END     SRT
```

The timing results are as follows, where

N = file size
T = sorting time in milliseconds
A = 100T/(N LOG2(N)).

Internal Sorting
11. Sorting Methods.
     50. Sifting: the Shell Sort.
          54. Assembly Language Comparison.

N=	1	2	4	7	11	18	29	46	72	114
T=	.055	.068	.086	.112	.148	.213	.390	.658	1.18	1.96
A=	5.46	3.38	1.07	.569	.389	.284	.277	.259	.265	.251

N=	179	280	439	686	1073	1677	2621
T=	3.41	6.60	10.7	20.1	30.7	53.1	99.1
A=	.255	.290	.277	.311	.284	.296	.333

The storage required is 136 bytes.
The result that the PL/1 program takes about 12 times as long to execute as the assembly language program is reasonably typical for programs of this type.

55. Partitioning: Quicksort.

We illustrate the notion of a partition sort using the file

(4 2 7 5 8 1 3 9 6).

Given any unsorted segment of a file we choose a bound element (the center item of the segment in this illustration, indicated by an underline), and form a lower segment consisting of those items less than or equal to the bound and an upper segment consisting of the items greater than the bound. The bound itself is left between these two segments. If, at any time, there is more than one unsorted segment left, we partition the shortest:

```
(4  2  7  5  8  1  3  9  6)
(4  2  7  5  1  3  6) 8 (9)
(4  2  7  5  1  3  6) 8  9
(4  2  1  3) 5 (7  6) 8  9
(4  2  1  3) 5 (6) 7  8  9
(4  2  1  3) 5  6  7  8  9
(1) 2 (4  3) 5  6  7  8  9
 1  2 (4  3) 5  6  7  8  9
 1  2 (3) 4  5  6  7  8  9
 1  2  3  4  5  6  7  8  9
```

A more formal description of the method is as follows.
Let X(p:q) be any segment of the file X(1:n). Let Y be any item in this segment. A permutation X'(p:q) of the items in the segment is called a __partition__ with respect to the bound Y if there exists a number b such that:

1) $p \leq b \leq q$,
2) $X'(b) = Y$,
3) if $p \leq i < b$ then $KX'(i) \leq KX'(b)$,
4) if $b < i \leq q$ then $KX'(b) < KX'(i)$.

If these conditions hold, then we write the partition as

Internal Sorting
11. Sorting Methods.
    55. Partitioning: Quicksort.

X'(p:b:q), calling X'(p:b-1) the lower and X'(b+1:q) the upper
segment of the partition. Either the lower or the upper segment
(or both, if p=q) may be empty.
    A complete partition sort works in the following way. Esta-
blish a pushdown list of ordered pairs (p,q) giving the bounds of
those segments X(p:q) which have not yet been sorted. At the
beginning of the sort of the file X(1:n) the pushdown list contains the single pair (1,n). Carry out the following recursive
procedure.
    If the pushdown list is empty the sort is finished; other-
wise pop up the top pair (p,q) from the pushdown list. If q-p<2
the segment X(p:q) is (either empty or) in sort; ignore it and
take the next pair. Form a partition X(p:b:q) of the segment
X(p:q). Push down the pairs (p,b-1) and (b+1,q) into the pushdown
list, the one representing the longer segment first. Now go back
and pop up the top pair.
    You will easily satisfy yourself that this algorithm ter-
minates, that when the pushdown list is empty the file is in
sort, and that the maximum number of pairs in the pushdown list
at any one time is [LOG2(n)]+1.
    A convenient algorithm for carrying out a partition is as
follows. Store the bound in an additional storage location Y and
move X(q) to the location it previously occupied, leaving an
"empty" location at q. Set a lower pointer i=p and an upper
pointer j=q.
    Move the lower pointer upward until an item X(i) is found
such that KX(i)>KY. Move X(i) to the empty location j, leaving an
empty location at i.
    Move the upper pointer downward until an item X(j) is found
such that KX(j)<KY. Move X(j) to the empty location i, leaving an
empty location at j again.
    Resume moving the pointer i, starting at location i+1 (i.e.,
just above the item that was moved into the empty location). And
so continue, using pointers i and j alternately, until j-i=1. Put
the item Y into the empty location b (which will be either j or
i=j-1, depending on which pointer is being moved). The partition
X(p:b:q) is now complete.
    Various versions of this process may be distinguished by the
method of choosing the bound item.
    Hoare (1961, 1962), the inventor of the method, used a
randomly selected item X(r) as bound in Quicksort, but suggested
also the median of a sample of items drawn from the segment.
    Scowen (1965) used X([(p+q)/2]) as bound in Quickersort, to
take advantage of any order existing in the segment. Boothroyd
(1967) gave an improved Algol version of Quickersort. Frazer
(1969, 1970) uses quantiles of a large sample of items in Samplesort to provide several successive bounds.
    Hoare suggests that segments of length less than some small
number m be sorted by an alternative process rather than being
further partitioned.

Internal Sorting
11. Sorting Methods.
    55. Partitioning: Quicksort.

Van Emden (1970, 1970b) shows that the number of comparisons required is of the form

A n LOG2(n),

where the coefficient A is 1.386 for Hoare's method, diminishing asymptotically toward 1 as the bound is taken as the median of a larger and larger sample.

Hoare's method (with refinements discussed below) is probably the best compromise for an internal sorting routine. It requires 2 LOG2(n) locations of additional storage for the pushdown list, compares favorably with other comparative methods in timing, and requires a program of moderate complexity. We therefore look at it in some detail.

The logical parallel between partitioning and the ancestral sort (par. 28) should be noticed. The bound Y corresponds to a node in the tree and the lower and upper segments correspond to the two subtrees descending from this node.

56. Original Quicksort.

The idea of sorting by successive partitions is due to Hoare (1961, 1962) in the algorithm called Quicksort.

Improvements, as discussed below, were suggested by Hibbard (1962a) and by Scowen (1965) in Quickersort.

The first improvement has to do with the management of the pushdown list required to keep track of the segments that have not yet been sorted. Each partition produces two segments, a lower segment and an upper segment, either of which may happen to be longer than the other. Hoare saved always the lower segment while he sorted the upper one, regardless of which segment was longer. This requires only one number in the pushdown list for each saved segment, but the number of saved segments could, in bad cases, be almost as big as the file size n. The Algol recursive subroutine feature was used, so that the pushdown list does not appear explicitly in the program.

Hibbard, on the other hand, saved always the longer segment, whether lower or upper, while he sorted the shorter. This requires two numbers in the pushdown list for each segment saved, but ensures that the number of saved segments is never greater than LOG2(n).

We, like Scowen, follow Hibbard in this storage saving. The choice has no effect on the number of comparisons and replacements required, and almost none on the sorting time.

The second point has to do with the choice of bound item. For partitioning the segment X(p:q), Hoare chooses a random item X(r) as bound. Hibbard chooses the item X(p) as bound. Scowen chooses the item X((p+q)/2) as bound, to take advantage of any bias that may already exist in the file. For a random file of the type used here, this choice has no appreciable effect on the sorting time. We choose X(q).

Internal Sorting
11. Sorting Methods.
     55. Partitioning: Quicksort.
          56. Original Quicksort.

     The procedure then looks like this.

```
SRT:   PROC(N); /* ORIGINAL QUICKSORT */
       DCL(N,P,LV(16),UV(16),LP,UP,Y) FIXED BIN(15);
       LV(1) = 1;                  /* INITIALIZE PUSHDOWN LIST */
       UV(1) = N;
       P = 1;
SRTB:  IF P<1 THEN RETURN;    /* PARTITION NEXT SEGMENT */
SRTC:  IF UV(P)-LV(P)<1 THEN DO;
          P = P - 1;
          GO TO SRTB;
          END;
       LP = LV(P) - 1;
       UP = UV(P);
       Y = X(UP);                        /* CHOOSE BOUND */
SRTD:  IF UP-LP<2 THEN GO TO SRTJ; /* MOVE LOWER POINTER */
       LP = LP + 1;
       IF X(LP)<=Y THEN GO TO SRTD;
       X(UP) = X(LP);
SRTF:  IF UP-LP<2 THEN GO TO SRTH; /* MOVE UPPER POINTER */
       UP = UP - 1;
       IF X(UP)>=Y THEN GO TO SRTF;
       X(LP) = X(UP);
       GO TO SRTD;
SRTH:  UP = UP - 1;                       /* FINISH UP */
SRTJ:  X(UP) = Y;
       IF UP-LV(P)<UV(P)-UP THEN DO;
          LV(P+1) = LV(P);
          UV(P+1) = UP - 1;
          LV(P) = UP + 1;
          END;
       ELSE DO;
          LV(P+1) = UP + 1;
          UV(P+1) = UV(P);
          UV(P) = UP - 1;
          END;
       P = P + 1;
       GO TO SRTC;
       END SRT;
```

     The timing results are as follows, where

     N = file size
     T = sorting time in milliseconds
     A = $100T/(N \, LOG2(N))$
     C = number of comparisons
     R = number of replacements.
     A superscript means multiplication by that power of 10.

Internal Sorting
11. Sorting Methods.
    55. Partitioning: Quicksort.
      56. Original Quicksort.

N=	1	2	4	7	11	18	29	46	72	114
T=	.073	.117	.164	.242	.416	.687	1.13	1.94	3.32	5.53
A=	7.28	5.85	2.05	1.23	1.09	.915	.805	.764	.746	.710
C=	0.00	1.00	4.90	13.3	29.4	59.7	119.	230.	430.	762.
R=	0.00	2.60	6.75	13.2	24.1	45.7	82.7	144.	242.	426.

N=	179	280	439	686	1073	1677	2621	4096	6400	10000
T=	9.37	15.4	25.9	42.7	71.1	119.	194.	323.	526.	870.
A=	.700	.677	.672	.660	.658	.663	.652	.656	.650	.655
C=	1411	2325	4117	6963	1197[1]	2022[1]	3362[1]	5731[1]	9429[1]	1567[2]
R=	708.	1195	1992	3328	5521	9104	1498[1]	2447[1]	3997[1]	6508[1]

The storage required is 932 bytes.

---
57. Van Emden's Modification.

    Instead of choosing a single bound for partitioning the segment X(p:q), van Emden (1970, 1970b) chooses an upper and lower bound, which are changed as necessary during the process to ensure that no item of the segment lies between them. This has the effect of making the upper and lower segments of the partition more nearly equal in size.
    The procedure looks like this.

```
SRT:   PROC(N); /* VAN EMDEN */
       DCL (N,P,LV(16),UV(16),LP,UP,XL,XU,Y) FIXED BIN(15);
       LV(1) = 1;              /* INITIALIZE PUSHDOWN LIST */
       UV(1) = N;
       P = 1;
SRTB:  IF P<1 THEN RETURN;     /* DO ONE PARTITION */
SRTC:  LP = LV(P);             /* SET POINTERS */
       UP = UV(P);
       IF UP-LP<1 THEN DO;     /* TEST FOR LENGTH ONE */
         P = P - 1;
         GO TO SRTB;
         END;
       IF X(LP)>X(UP) THEN DO; /* TEST END ITEMS */
         Y = X(LP);
         X(LP) = X(UP);
         X(UP) = Y;
         END;
       IF UP-LP=1 THEN DO;     /* CHECK LENGTH TWO */
         P = P - 1;
         GO TO SRTB;
         END;
       XL = X(LP);             /* SET TENTATIVE BOUNDS */
       XU = X(UP);
SRTD:  IF UP-LP<2 THEN GO TO SRTJ; /* MOVE LOWER POINTER */
       LP = LP + 1;
       IF X(LP)<=XL THEN GO TO SRTD;
```

Internal Sorting
11. Sorting Methods.
    55. Partitioning: Quicksort.
        57. Van Emden's Modification.


```
 SRTF: IF UP-LP<2 THEN GO TO SRTH; /* MOVE UPPER POINTER */
       UP = UP - 1;
       IF X(UP)>=XU THEN GO TO SRTF;
       IF X(LP)>X(UP) THEN DO;       /* BOTH POINTERS BLOCKED */
         Y = X(LP);
         X(LP)  = X(UP);
         X(UP)  = Y;
         END;
       IF X(LP)>XL THEN DO;  /* CHANGE BOUNDS IF NECESSARY */
         XL = X(LP);
         END;
       IF X(UP)<XU THEN DO;
         XU = X(UP);
         END;
       GO TO SRTD;
 SRTH: LP = LP - 1;
       UP = UP - 1;
 SRTJ: IF LP-LV(P)<UV(P)-UP THEN DO; /* UPDATE PUSHDOWN LIST */
         LV(P+1) = LV(P);
         UV(P+1) = LP;
         LV(P)  = UP;
         END;
       ELSE DO;
         LV(P+1) = UP;
         UV(P+1) = UV(P);
         UV(P)  = LP;
         END;
       P = P + 1;
       GO TO SRTC;
       END SRT;
```

The timing results are as follows, where

N = file size
T = sorting time in milliseconds
A = 100T/(N LOG2(N))
C = number of comparisons
R = number of replacements.
A superscript means multiplication by that power of 10.

N=	1	2	4	7	11	18	29	46	72	114
T=	.088	.094	.169	.260	.478	.814	1.38	2.37	3.98	6.73
A=	8.84	4.68	2.11	1.32	1.26	1.08	.978	.934	.895	.864
C=	0.00	1.00	6.82	20.5	45.3	97.1	193.	364.	657.	1184
R=	0.00	1.80	9.32	23.0	45.6	84.4	156.	269.	463.	790.

Internal Sorting
11. Sorting Methods.
55. Partitioning: Quicksort.
57. Van Emden's Modification.

N=	179	280	439	686	1073	1677	2621	4096	6400	10000
T=	11.3	19.0	32.1	53.2	87.7	144.	236.	392.	634.	1037
A=	.842	.837	.833	.824	.812	.802	.794	.797	.784	.780
C=	2070	3580	6161	1048^1	1766^1	2972^1	4946^1	8290^1	1360^2	2248^2
R=	1318	2209	3651	6013	9888	1614^1	2623^1	4228^1	6803^1	1085^2

The storage required is 1124 bytes.
The method is not sequence-preserving.

---
58. Samplesort.

Hoare suggested that the bound for each partition be chosen as the median of a sample of size s drawn from the segment to be partitioned, in order to keep the lengths of the two segments resulting from the partition as nearly equal as possible.

Clearly the sample size s should depend on the length of the segment to be partitioned, a larger sample being used for longer segments.

Frazer and McKellar (1969) exploit this notion in Samplesort.

Their paper does not give all details of their method, which in fact was intended primarily for the internal phase of an external sort. The method described here is somewhat modified to fit the present framework.

The method proceeds in three main steps:

1) Selection of a sample of size s,
2) Sorting of this sample,
3) Sorting of the main file, using items from the sample as partition bounds, as long as they last.

The sample size s is always one less than a power of two and is determined approximately by the formula

$$n = (s+1)[\,LOG\,(s+1) - 0.51\,]$$

where 'LOG' means the natural logarithm. From figure 2 of the cited paper it appears that it is safer to take s too small than too large. Also for very small files the additional complexity of drawing the sample is not worthwhile, and the midpoint of the segment is used as bound.

Frazer and McKellar draw the sample randomly from the initial file. We take, instead, a set of equally spaced items. This simplifies the program and improves the method's inherent ability to take account of distribution bias in the original file.

The items of the sample are copied into a working file Z(1:s) for sorting and later use, but are also left in their original places in the original file, to be sorted with the other items in step 3. This means that additional storage is needed for

Internal Sorting
11. Sorting Methods.
    55. Partitioning: Quicksort.
        58. Samplesort.

the temporary file Z and that the sample items are, in effect, sorted twice. If this is the internal phase of an external sort then the sample could be moved to the beginning of the original file X (by appropriate interchanges of items) and then merged with the rest of the file, after this remainder has been sorted, during the output phase.

But for a straight internal sort, this final merge has to be done in place, and the extra time required does not seem a fair price to pay for the saving of storage.

When the sample has been selected into $Z(1:s)$, it is sorted by Scowen's Quickersort.

A faster method, such as Samplesort or the method of par. 62, could be used instead, but hardly seems justified.

The main file is now sorted by partitioning. The sample median $Z((s+1)/2)$ is used as a partition bound for the first segment $X(1:n)$ to give the upper and lower segments $X(1:p-1)$, $X(p+1,n)$. These are stored in the pushdown list, larger one first, in the usual manner. The quartile items $Z((s+1)/4)$ and $Z(3(s+1)/4)$ are used as partition bounds for these segments, respectively, when their turn comes to be sorted. And so continue, using the correct item of Z for the partition bound of each segment, if there is still one left for this section of the file and using the midpoint of the segment if there is not.

This requires a third entry, say MV, for each segment in the pushdown list, to remember which item of Z is to be used as partition bound for that segment when its turn comes. And this quantity must be computed for the upper and lower segments of each partition at the time these segments are determined. If no item of the sample remains for this use, we set $MV=0$ for the segment to so indicated.

The procedure is as follows.

```
SRT:   PROC(N); /* SAMPLESORT */
       DCL (N,Y,Z(1023),I,S,J,W,M1,M2) FIXED BIN(15);
       DCL (P,LV(16),UV(16),MV(16)) FIXED BIN(15);
       DCL (LP,UP) FIXED BIN(15);
       DCL SV(6) FIXED BIN(15) STATIC
               INIT(15,31,63,127,255,511);
       DCL NV(6) FIXED BIN(15) STATIC
               INIT(98,233,566,1287,2930,6580);
       IF N<36 THEN DO;        /* TEST SMALL FILE */
         MV(1) = 0;
         GO TO SRL;
         END;
       DO I = 1 TO 6;          /* FIND SAMPLE SIZE */
         IF N< NV(I) THEN DO;
           S = SV(I);
           GO TO SRB;
           END;
         END;
```

Internal Sorting
11. Sorting Methods.
    55. Partitioning: Quicksort.
      58. Samplesort.

```
          S = 1023;
  SRB:    J = N/S;                      /* SELECT THE SAMPLE */
          DO I = 1 TO S;
             Z(I) = X(I*J);
             END;
          LV(1) = 1;                    /* SORT THE SAMPLE */
          UV(1) = S;
          P = 1;
  SRD:    IF P<1 THEN GO TO SRK;
  SRE:    IF UV(P)-LV(P)<1 THEN DO;
             P = P - 1;
             GO TO SRD;
             END;
          LP = LV(P) - 1;
          UP = UV(P);
          J = (LP+UP+1)/2;
          Y = Z(J);
          Z(J) = Z(UP);
  SRF:    IF UP-LP<2 THEN GO TO SRJ;
          LP = LP + 1;
          IF Z(LP)<=Y THEN GO TO SRF;
          Z(UP) = Z(LP);
  SRG:    IF UP-LP<2 THEN GO TO SRH;
          UP = UP - 1;
          IF Z(UP)>=Y THEN GO TO SRG;
          Z(LP) = Z(UP);
          GO TO SRF;
  SRH:    UP = UP - 1;
  SRJ:    Z(UP) = Y;
          IF UP-LV(P)<UV(P)-UP THEN DO;
             LV(P+1) = LV(P);
             UV(P+1) = UP - 1;
             LV(P) = UP + 1;
             END;
          ELSE DO;
             LV(P+1) = UP + 1;
             UV(P+1) = UV(P);
             UV(P) = UP - 1;
             END;
          P = P + 1;
          GO TO SRE;
  SRK:    MV(1) = (S+1)/2;              /* SORT MAIN FILE */
  SRL:    LV(1) = 1;
          UV(1) = N;
          P = 1;
  SRM:    IF P<1 THEN RETURN;
  SRN:    IF UV(P)-LV(P)<1 THEN DO;
             P = P - 1;
             GO TO SRM;
             END;
```

Internal Sorting
11. Sorting Methods.
    55. Partitioning: Quicksort.
       58. Samplesort.

```
          LP = LV(P) - 1;
          UP = UV(P);
          IF MV(P)>0 THEN Y = Z(MV(P));
                    ELSE Y = X(UP);
          W = X(UP);
SRP:      IF UP-LP<2 THEN GO TO SRS;
          LP = LP + 1;
          IF X(LP)<=Y THEN GO TO SRP;
          X(UP) = X(LP);
SRQ:      IF UP-LP<2 THEN GO TO SRR;
          UP = UP - 1;
          IF X(UP)> Y THEN GO TO SRQ;
          X(LP) = X(UP);
          GO TO SRP;
SRR:      UP = UP - 1;
SRS:      X(UP) = W;
          IF W<Y THEN UP = UP + 1;
          IF UP>UV(P) THEN DO;
SRU:        MV(P) = 0;
            LP = LV(P) - 1;
            UP = UV(P);
            W, Y = X(UP);
            GO TO SRP;
            END;
          IF W=Y THEN I = 1;
                  ELSE I = 0;
          IF (UP=LV(P))&(I=0) THEN GO TO SRU;
          IF (MV(P)=0)|(MOD(MV(P),4)¬=0) THEN DO;
            M1, M2 = 0;
            END;
          ELSE DO;
            J = 8;
            DO WHILE(MOD(MV(P),J)=0);
              J = J + J;
              END;
            J = J/4;
            M1 = MV(P) - J;
            M2 = MV(P) + J;
            END;
          IF UP-LV(P)<UV(P)-UP THEN DO;
            LV(P+1) = LV(P);
            UV(P+1) = UP - 1;
          LV(P) = UP + I;
            MV(P) = M2;
            MV(P+1) = M1;
            END;
          ELSE DO;
          LV(P+1) = UP + I;
            UV(P+1) = UV(P);
            UV(P) = UP - 1;
```

Internal Sorting
11. Sorting Methods.
   55. Partitioning: Quicksort.
    58. Samplesort.

```
      MV(P) = M1;
      MV(P+1) = M2;
      END;
    P = P + 1;
    GO TO SRN;
    END SRT;
```

The timing results are as follows, where

N = file size
T = sorting time in milliseconds
A = $100T/(N \, LOG2(N))$
C = number of comparisons
R = number of replacements.
A superscript means multiplication by that power of 10.

N=	1	2	4	7	11	18	29	46	72	114
T=	.411	.455	.585	.687	.924	1.33	2.02	4.02	5.83	9.97
A=	41.1	22.7	7.32	3.50	2.43	1.77	1.43	1.58	1.31	1.28
C=	0.00	3.00	9.65	21.5	43.1	83.2	157.	331.	538.	990.
R=	0.00	3.60	9.12	17.3	31.0	57.4	102.	263.	385.	704.

N=	179	280	439	686	1073	1677	2621	4096	6400	10000
T=	15.0	24.9	38.3	63.8	99.2	167.	255.	422.	667.	1090
A=	1.12	1.09	.993	.988	.919	.928	.856	.858	.825	.821
C=	1615	2823	4575	7862	1265^{1}	2147^{1}	3438^{1}	5775^{1}	9269^{1}	1543^{2}
R=	1043	1851	2999	4839	7382	1263^{1}	1937^{1}	3272^{1}	5054^{1}	8453^{1}

The storage required is 2200 bytes plus 2s for the working file Z.
The method is not sequence-preserving.

59. Equal Keys.

A problem arises if the file consists of sets of items with equal keys. Consider the limiting case in which all items have the same key. Then the upper segment of each partition is empty, and the size of the unsorted segment is reduced only by 1 at the cost of q-p-1 comparisons, so that the timing order is n^2 for this case, instead of n log n as it is for distinct keys.
Since many files have several items with equal keys and since repeated partitioning will then produce segments that approach the limiting case of equal keys, it is expedient to make a special provision for this case.
If the upper segment of a partition is null, then the bound was one of the maximum items in the segment and it is then likely that other items in the segment have the same key. In this case, then, we make a second pass over the segment to collect all the items with this maximal key and put them in the upper segment, putting the other items in the lower segment. The upper segment,

Internal Sorting
11. Sorting Methods.
    55. Partitioning: Quicksort.
        59. Equal Keys.

of course, is then in sort and need not be added to the pushdown
list.
    With this modification, the time required to sort n items
decreases rather than increases as the number of distinct keys
decreases, with no great timing penalty when all keys are distinct.
    Any of the partitioning methods can be provided with this
separate pass to collect equal items when one of the segments
resulting from the partition is null (or contains a single item,
in van Emden's method). But in a segment of length m, this will
happen with probability 1/m even if there are no equal items, and
the collection pass is then a useless expense.
    Taking the bound as a median of a sample size greater than
one reduces the probability of this event. For a sample of length
3, for example, it will not occur unless two items of the sample
have the same key, and this is the maximal key for the segment.
This will never happen unless there are in fact equal items, and
is very unlikely unless there are many equal items.

60. Sample Size for Choice of Bound.

    We would like to choose the bound for each partition in such
a way that the lengths of the two resulting segments are as
nearly equal as possible, since the dependence of the timing
function T(n) on n is stronger than linear. To achieve this, we
might choose a sample of size 2k+1 from the segment, sort this
sample, and choose its median as the partition bound.
    Of course it takes some time to sort the sample and execute
the overhead of the more complicated program, and it is therefore
not clear a priori what the optimal sample size is.
    The procedure was therefore programmed with k as a parame-
ter, the sample being sorted by ranking. It turned out, under the
particular assumptions used (par. 8) that a sample size of 3
(i.e., k=1) gives as fast a sort as a larger sample, at least for
n≤10,000. Perhaps for very large files (n>50,000, say) the
question should be looked at again.
    Sander-Cederlof (1970) uses a sample size of 3 in Supersort,
and also uses a ranking sort for segments of 11 items or less.
    The use of a sample size greater than 1 reduces the proba-
bility that the special pass to collect equal items will be made
when it is not appropriate.
    Hurwitz (1971) shows that increasing k (past 1 or 2) has
more effect in reducing the variance of sorting times than in
reducing the mean.

Internal Sorting
11. Sorting Methods.
    55. Partitioning: Quicksort.
        60. Sample Size for Choice of Bound.

---

61. Treatment of Small Segments.

    Hoare suggests that segments of length less than or equal to
m should be sorted by an alternate method rather than by being
further partitioned, where m is a number whose optimal value
remains to be determined.

    The most reasonable proposal for sorting these short seg-
ments is ranking. Of course, for m=2 a single comparison suffices
with any method.

    It turns out that, under the experimental assumptions used
here, the time for a partition sort with m=2 is not appreciably
greater than for a ranking sort for any value of n. With m=1, the
ranking sort is faster for n<10. Hence, it appears that m=2 is a
reasonable choice.

    Of course if a sample size greater than 1 is used for deter-
mining the bound, then m must be taken at least as large as this
sample size minus one.

---

62. Improved Procedure.

    The procedure with the suggested improvements, namely a
sample size of three and a special pass for equal items if necessary, looks like this.

```
SRT:    PROC(N); /* IMPROVED QUICKSORT */
        DCL (N,LP,UP,P,LV(16),UV(16),M,C,Y) FIXED BIN(15);
        LV(1) = 1;              /* INITIALIZE PUSHDOWN LIST */
        UV(1) = N;
        P = 1;
STB:    IF P<1 THEN RETURN;     /* PARTITION ONE SEGMENT */
STC:    LP = LV(P);
        UP = UV(P);
        M = UP - LP + 1;
        IF M<2 THEN DO;
          P = P - 1;
          GO TO STB;
          END;
        IF M=2 THEN DO;
          IF X(LP)>X(UP) THEN DO;
            Y = X(LP);
            X(LP) = X(UP);
            X(UP) = Y;
            END;
          P = P - 1;
          GO TO STB;
          END;
        C = (LP+UP)/2;          /* CHOOSE BOUND */
        IF M<10 THEN GO TO STD;
        IF X(LP) <=X(C) THEN DO;
```

Internal Sorting
11. Sorting Methods.
    55. Partitioning: Quicksort.
        62. Improved Procedure.

```
          IF X(C)<=X(UP) THEN GO TO STD;
          ELSE DO;
            IF X(LP)<=X(UP) THEN C = UP;
                            ELSE C = LP;
            GO TO STD;
            END;
          END;
        ELSE DO;
          IF X(UP)<=X(C) THEN GO TO STD;
          ELSE DO;
            IF X(LP)<=X(UP) THEN C = LP;
                            ELSE C = UP;
            GO TO STD;
            END;
          END;
STD:  Y = X(C);
      X(C) = X(UP);
      LP = LP - 1;
STF:  IF UP-LP<2 THEN GO TO STK;   /* MOVE LOWER POINTER */
      LP = LP + 1;
      IF X(LP)<=Y THEN GO TO STF;
      X(UP) = X(LP);
STH:  IF UP-LP<2 THEN GO TO STJ;   /* MOVE UPPER POINTER */
      UP = UP - 1;
      IF X(UP)>Y THEN GO TO STH;
      X(LP) = X(UP);
      GO TO STF;
STJ:  UP = UP - 1;
STK:  IF UP=UV(P) THEN DO;         /* TEST FOR EQUAL ITEMS */
        LP = LV(P) - 1;
STL:    IF UP-LP<2 THEN GO TO STQ;
        LP = LP + 1;
        IF X(LP)<Y THEN GO TO STL;
        X(UP) = X(LP);
STN:    IF UP-LP<2 THEN GO TO STP;
        UP = UP - 1;
        IF X(UP)>=Y THEN GO TO STN;
        X(LP) = X(UP);
        GO TO STL;
STP:    UP = UP - 1;
STQ:    X(UP) = Y;
        IF UP = LV(P) THEN DO;
          P = P - 1;
          GO TO STB;
          END;
        UV(P) = UP - 1;
        GO TO STC;
        END;
      /* IF UPPER SEGMENT NOT EMPTY, STORE BOTH SEGMENTS */
      X(UP) = Y;
```

Internal Sorting
11. Sorting Methods.
    55. Partitioning: Quicksort.
        62. Improved Procedure.


```
    IF UP-LV(P)<UV(P)-UP THEN DO;
      LV(P+1) = LV(P);
      UV(P+1) = UP - 1;
      LV(P) = UP + 1;
      END;
    ELSE DO;
      LV(P+1) = UP + 1;
      UV(P+1) = UV(P);
      UV(P) = UP - 1;
      END;
    P = P + 1;
    GO TO STC;
    END SRT;
```

The timing results are as follows, where

N = file size
T = sorting time in milliseconds
A = $100T/(N \ LOG2(N))$
C = number of comparisons
R = number of replacements.
A superscript means multiplication by that power of 10.

N=	1	2	4	7	11	18	29	46	72	114
T=	.078	.078	.177	.262	.426	.736	1.20	2.00	3.28	5.56
A=	7.80	3.90	2.21	1.34	1.12	.980	.849	.787	.739	.714
C=	0.00	1.00	5.70	15.7	32.6	66.6	128.	238.	422.	749.
R=	0.00	1.80	6.90	15.2	28.2	51.9	93.5	161.	272.	468.

N=	179	280	439	686	1073	1677	2621	4096	6400	10000
T=	9.26	15.4	25.5	42.2	69.8	114.	187.	305.	498.	801.
A=	.692	.676	.662	.653	.646	.634	.629	.620	.615	.603
C=	1311	2259	3869	6575	1126^1	1866^1	3126^1	5178^1	8583^1	1423^2
R=	781.	1315	2184	3620	5967	9857	1610^1	2630^1	4276^1	6895^1

The storage required is 1576 bytes.
The method is not sequence-preserving.

----
63. Conclusions.

The best overall choice of a comparative method for internal sorting now appears to be a partition sort, with bound chosen as the middle item of a three-item sample, with segments of length 2 sorted ad hoc, and with the special pass to collect equal keys when the upper segment of a partition is empty.
This method is not sequence-preserving.

Internal Sorting
11. Sorting Methods.
   55. Partitioning: Quicksort.
     63. Conclusions.

64. Maximum Sorting Time.

Hibbard (1963) conjectures that, for any comparative method of sorting by interchange of items, the maximum sorting time is of order n^2. This conjecture holds for Scowen's method. We simply choose a file such that the item selected for the bound is always the one with the largest key. The first few files in this sequence are:

```
2,1
2,3,1
2,4,3,1
2,4,5,3,1
2,4,6,5,3,1
etc.
```

Examples can be found, though with slightly more work, to confirm the conjecture when a sample size greater than 1 is used to select the bound, and when segments of length greater than 2 are sorted by an alternative method.

I have not found an example that verifies the conjecture for Shell's method.

65. Treesort 3.

The original Treesort algorithm (Floyd 1962) used 2n additional storage locations, and is not considered in detail here. The improved version (Floyd 1964) uses no additional locations, but rather uses the ideas of Williams (1964) to build the tree in place, without pointers.

We consider the file X(n) itself as an incomplete binary vector tree (par. 10), that is: for the file X(1:n) we call any location i the _father_ of the two _brothers_ 2i and 2i+1. Each of these is again the father of two brothers, and so on, until the limit n of the file is exceeded. Thus, any location $i \leq n/2$ is the root of a subtree of the complete tree with root at location 1.

Treesort provides a procedure which _shifts_ the item at the root of a subtree upward (by exchanges across single links of the tree) until its key is less than or equal to that of any of its ancestors within the resulting subtree. This shifting procedure is systematically called until the subtree rooted on every location except i=1 has this descending property.

A final pass then exchanges the items into sort order.

The program for doing this is quite compact and the time required is of the order of n log n. For the test case described in par. 8, this method is not quite so fast as Quicksort (which, however, does require additional storage locations). The method is not sequence-preserving.

The procedure used for the timing tests is as follows:

Internal Sorting
11. Sorting Methods.
    65. Treesort 3.


```
SRT:    PROC(N); /* TREESORT 3 */
        DCL SRU ENTRY(FIXED BIN(15),FIXED BIN(15)); /* SHIFT */
        DCL (N,Y,I) FIXED BIN(15);
        DO I = N/2 BY -1 TO 2;
          CALL SRU(I,N);
          END;
        DO I = N BY -1 TO 2;
          CALL SRU(1,I);
          Y = X(1);
          X(1) = X(I);
          X(I) = Y;
          END;
        RETURN;
SRU:    PROC(R,N); /* SHIFT ROOT UPWARD IN ITS TREE */
        DCL (R,N,I,J) FIXED BIN(15);
        I = R;
        Y = X(I);
SRUH:   J = 2*I;
        IF J<=N THEN DO;
          IF J<N THEN DO;
            IF X(J+1)>X(J) THEN J = J + 1;
            END;
          IF X(J)>Y THEN DO;
            X(I) = X(J);
            I = J;
            GO TO SRUH;
            END;
          END;
        X(I) = Y;
        RETURN;
        END SRU;
        END SRT;
```

The timing results for this procedure are as follows, where

N = file size
T = sorting time in milliseconds
A = 100T/(N LOG2(N))
C = number of comparisons
R = number of replacements.
A superscript means multiplication by that power of 10.

N=	1	2	4	7	11	18	29	46	72	114
T=	.068	.114	.267	.481	.882	1.56	2.67	4.93	7.88	13.3
A=	6.76	5.72	3.35	2.45	2.32	2.08	1.89	1.94	1.77	1.71
C=	0.00	1.00	6.45	19.8	45.5	97.8	194.	371.	674.	1211
R=	0.00	5.40	20.2	42.9	78.6	145.	255.	441.	741.	1247

Internal Sorting
11. Sorting Methods.
    65. Treesort 3.

N=	179	280	439	686	1073	1677	2621	4096	6400	10000
T=	22.4	37.2	62.2	103.	167.	278.	453.	747.	1216	1963
A=	1.67	1.63	1.61	1.59	1.55	1.54	1.52	1.52	1.50	1.48
C=	2142	3692	6373	1085^1	1831^1	3085^1	5159^1	8566^1	1425^2	2354^2
R=	2079	3424	5664	9297	1521^1	2490^1	4061^1	6597^1	1074^2	1742^2

The storage required for this procedure is 1076 bytes.

----
66. Summary of Results.

The results of this section are summarized in the following
table. The double column marked 'CODES' shows 'C' for comparative
methods or 'NC' for non-comparative (integral) methods and 'SP'
for sequence-preserving methods or 'NSP' for non-sequence-preser-
ving methods. The storage required is shown in the column labeled
'BYTES'; the program storage and the additional storage (if any)
for sorting 10,000 halfword integers are shown separately. The
time in seconds for sorting 10,000 items is shown in the last
column; values marked with an asterisk were extrapolated from the
actual rest results.

METHOD	CODES	BYTES	SECONDS
Address (par. 13)	NC| SP	1034+ 60000	.415
Pigeon Hole (par. 18)	NC|NSP	1418+ 3252	1.379
Upward Radix (par. 19)	NC| SP	690+ 40000	4.43*
Downward Radix (par. 20)	NC|NSP	1276	4.40*
Natural Merge (par. 24)	C| SP	1830+ 80000	3.130
Straight Merge (par. 25)	C| SP	1602+ 20000	1.332
Merge, opt. strings (par. 26)	C| SP	2122+ 20000	1.136
Chain Merge (par. 27)	C| SP	1852+ 44000	1.74
Ancestral (par. 28)	C| SP	1058+ 80000	2.21
Ancestral, based (par. 29)	C| SP	1068+160000	4.72*
Counting (par. 31)	C| SP	590+ 40000	317*
Count and Interchange (par. 32)	C| SP	634+ 20000	396*
Tournament, surrogate (par. 35)	C| SP	1550+ 85534	3.35
Tournament, direct (par. 36)	C| SP	1462+ 65534	3.049
Transposition (par. 38)	C| SP	528	651*
Alternating Trans. (par. 39)	C| SP	784	480*
Odd-even Transp. (par. 40)	C| SP	672	372*
Bubble (par. 41)	C| SP	612	357*
Bubble, no switch (par. 42)	C| SP	540	396*
Funnel (par. 43)	C| SP	816	328*
Minima (par. 44)	C| SP	572	325*
Ranking, Direct (par. 45)	C| SP	568	179*
Ranking, Binary (par. 46)	C| SP	652	82.8*
P-Operator (par. 48)	C|NSP	2938	120.4*
Bose-Hibbard (par. 49)	C|NSP	2476	5500*
Shell (par. 51)	C|NSP	692	323*
Shell-Frank (par. 52)	C|NSP	744	287*
Shell-Hibbard (par. 53)	C|NSP	788	337*
Original Quicksort (par. 56)	C|NSP	932	.870
Van Emden Sort (par. 57)	C|NSP	1124	1.037
Improved Quicksort (par. 62)	C|NSP	1576	.801
Treesort 3 (par. 65)	C|NSP	1076	1.96

67. A Standard Sort.

The preceding discussion indicates that a general purpose internal sorting routine should be based on Quicksort (par. 62) with bounds chosen from a sample of three items.

The next question to be answered is how to make the routine work for the variety of files met in practice. We consider this question next.

68. File Parameters.

A general purpose sorting routine must be able to handle any (reasonable) file structure and any key mapping function appropriate to that structure. It must therefore have enough information about the file to permit comparison of items and movement of items (or their surrogates) from place to place.

The main ways of making this information available to the procedure are:

1) As subroutine arguments (par. 69),
2) By subsubroutines (par. 70),
3) By program generation (par. 71),
4) By compile-time specialization (par. 72).

Let us consider each of these in turn.

69. Use of Subroutine Arguments.

A routine for the calculation of a mathematical function, such as the square root, is usually written as a fixed closed subroutine with the input (or inputs) as argument(s).

This approach is cumbersome for a general purpose sort routine because most languages (and PL/1 in particular) do not have a convenient provision for passing the attributes of structures, and also because the variety of sorting key transformations is so great that a very large number of arguments would be required for adequate generality. The long resulting calling sequences are prodigal of memory, and the code within the subroutine to test and handle all these arguments takes both memory and execution time.

70. Use of Subsubroutines.

The only information about the file actually needed by the sort subroutine is that which is necessary to compare two elements and to move an element (or its surrogate) from one place to another.

We could, therefore, require the user to write PL/1 procedures to carry out these functions and pass the names of these procedures as arguments to the sort procedure.

Unfortunately these ad hoc procedures are called in inner

Internal Sorting
67. A Standard Sort.
    68. File Parameters.
        70. Use of Subsubroutines.

loops of the sort procedure, and the PL/1 calling sequence is so
slow that the time becomes prohibitive. Preliminary tests indicate that this approach may be slower by a factor of ten than the
method described in par. 72.

It is not usually good practice, in PL/1, to use short
closed subroutines in inner loops.

71. Program Generation.

A program generator is a program which accepts parameters as
inputs and then generates a program to carry out some function
(such as sorting) in a way carefully tailored to these parameters.

Sort generators have been constructed in profusion over the
years, but mostly for external sorting. This is still an attrac-
tive approach if the applications involved merit the extra time
and effort required to generate the program in assembly language.

For adequate treatment of the variety of data structures
available in PL/1, the number of parameters required would be
very large and the sort generator becomes a major programming
task.

Also, a special preliminary run for program generation must
be made before the main program (which uses the sort routine) is
compiled.

72. Compile-Time Specialization.

The final possibility is similar to that discussed in par.
70, except that open routines are used instead of closed ones to
avoid the calling overhead. These open routines are written by
the user as compile-time procedures, and become part of the sort
routine at compile time.

This approach has the disadvantage that if several different
structures are to be sorted in the same main program, then
several copies of the sort routine must be included. Fortunately
this situation does not seem to arise very often in practice.

The approach has the advantage of complete flexibility, in
that all access to the file is via the compile-time procedures,
and these are written to suit whatever file and key structure is
involved, whether the sort is direct or by surrogate.

73. The Compile Time Procedures.

The sort procedure is included in the library in a skeletal
form, which is specialized to meet your needs at compile time. In
order to cause this specialization, you must write several compile time procedures, as described in the following sections, to
precede the INCLUDE statement that brings the skeletal procedure
in from the library.

The PL/1 statements generated by these compile time proce-

Internal Sorting
67. A Standard Sort.
    73. The Compile Time Procedures.

dures are subject to only two restrictions:

1. Do not begin any names with an at-sign '@'; this avoids
    conflicts with names used in the skeletal procedure.
2. Labels must be treated in a special way (par. 77).

The several compile time procedures are next discussed.

---

74. $S(I): Set a Symbol.

For convenience in writing and using the other macros, you
will want to define a macro $S, which will construct a correct
symbol name.
    You must declare a temporary location, say Y, through which
to make the item interchanges. The call $S(*) is replaced with
this name, and the call $S(I) with the name X(I) of the indicated
file item, in the two following macros.
    The compile time coding is as follows:

```
% $S: PROC(I) RETURNS(CHAR) /* SET A SYMBOL */;
     DCL I CHAR;
     IF I = '*' THEN RETURN('Y');
     RETURN('X('||I||')');
%    END $S;
```

---

75. $R(I,J): Replace I-th Item by J-th.

This compile-time procedure causes the I-th item of the file
to be replaced by the J-th item of the file. The macro $S is
used, so that either argument of $R may be an asterisk denoting
the tempo Y. The compile-time code is as follows.

```
% $R: PROC(I,J) RETURNS(CHAR) /* REPLACE ITEM */;
     DCL (I,J) CHAR;
     RETURN($S(I)||'='||$S(J));
%    END $R;
```

---

76. $C(I,R,J,L): Compare Two Items.

The compile-time procedure $C generates the code to compare
two items, using a specified relation R, and jump to the label L
if the relation holds. The macro $S is used, so that either of
the arguments I,J may be an asterisk denoting the tempo Y. The
compile-time code required is as follows:

```
% $C: PROC(I,R,J,L) RETURNS(CHAR) /* COMPARE */;
     DCL (I,R,J,L) CHAR;
     RETURN('IF '||$S(I)||R||$S(J)||' THEN GO TO '||L);
%    END $C;
```

The simple example shown, of course, applies to the situa-

Internal Sorting
67. A Standard Sort.
    73. The Compile Time Procedures.
        76. $C(I,R,J,L): Compare Two Items.

tion in which the whole file item constitutes a single key. For a
sort using a more complex key structure, this comparison macro
becomes correspondingly more complicated.

77. Labels in Own Code.

The fourth argument of the comparison procedure $C (par.
76), although it acts like a label in the code generated by that
procedure, is explicitly excluded from the labels discussed in
this section.

The compile time procedures required to specialize the sort
procedure are usually so simple logically that the code they
generate will not require GO TO statements and the labels to
which they refer. If you do use such internal labels, however,
the following problem arises.

Each call of one of your compile time procedures copies into
the sort procedure being generated a sequence of PL/1 code, as
defined by that compile time procedure. If this sequence of code
contains a label, say 'ALFA', then each copy will contain this
label, and the compiler will issue a duplicate label alarm.

We require a mechanism, therefore, to make the name 'ALFA'
look different from one copy to the next, while remaining the
same throughout any one copy.

To this end, the sort skeleton uses a compile time variable
$M, initialized to 100, and a compile time procedure '$' so written that the symbol '$(ALFA)' is replaced by the symbol 'ALFAdd',
where 'dd' are the last two digits of the current value of $M.

Hence, if any of your compile time procedures uses a label
'ALFA', you must start it with the (compile time) statement

    $M=$M+1;

and then write '$(ALFA)' instead of 'ALFA' throughout the proce-
dure.

78. The Program.

The procedure is shown together with the own coding for the
simple example used throughout for timing comparisons. The portion stored in the library to be brought in by the INCLUDE
statement is indicated by comment lines.

```
SRT:   PROC(aLF,aUF); /* QUICKSORT WITH MACROS */
       DCL Y FIXED BIN(15);
% $S:  PROC(I) RETURNS(CHAR)   /* SET A SYMBOL */;
       DCL I CHAR;
       IF I = '*' THEN RETURN('Y');
       RETURN('X('||I||')');
%      END $S;
% $R:  PROC(I,J) RETURNS(CHAR) /* REPLACE ITEM */;
```

Internal Sorting
67. A Standard Sort.
   78. The Program.


```
        DCL (I,J)CHAR;
        RETURN($S(I)||'='||$S(J));
%       END $R;
%  $C: PROC(I,R,J,L) RETURNS(CHAR) /* COMPARE */;
        DCL (I,R,J,L)CHAR;
        RETURN('IF '||$S(I)||R||$S(J)||' THEN GO TO '||L);
%       END $C;


/* TEXT BROUGHT IN BY THE INCLUDE STATEMENT STARTS HERE */

%  DCL $S ENTRY(CHAR) RETURNS(CHAR);
%  DCL $R ENTRY(CHAR,CHAR) RETURNS(CHAR) /* REPLACE */;
%  DCL $C ENTRY(CHAR,CHAR,CHAR,CHAR)RETURNS(CHAR);
%  DCL $ ENTRY(CHAR)RETURNS(CHAR) /* CONVERT LABEL */;
%  DCL $M FIXED;
%      $M = 100;
%  $:  PROC(S) RETURNS(CHAR) /* SET LABEL */;
        DCL (S,C) CHAR;
        C = $M;
        RETURN(S||SUBSTR(C,7,2));
%       END $;
        DCL (@I,@M,@LF,@UF,@LL,@UL,@LI,@UI)    FIXED BIN(15);
        DCL (@P,@LV(20),@UV(20))FIXED BIN(15);
        @P = 1;                    /* INITIALIZE PUSHDOWN LIST */
        @LV(1) = @LF; @UV(1) = @UF;
@SA:    IF @P<1 THEN GO TO @SY; /* DO ONE SEGMENT */
        @LL = @LV(@P); @UL = @UV(@P);
        @M = @UL - @LL + 1;
        IF @M<2 THEN DO;
@SB:      @P = @P - 1;
          GO TO @SA;
          END;
        /* FIND BOUND AS MEDIAN OF THREE-ITEM SAMPLE. */
        @I = (@LL+@UL)/2;
        @UI = (@I+@UL+1)/2;
        $C(@I,<=,@UI,@SC);
        $R(*,@I); $R(@I,@UI); $R(@UI,*);
@SC:    IF @M=2 THEN GO TO @SB;
        @LI = (@LL+@I)/2;
        $C(@LI,<=,@I,@SD);
        $R(*,@LI); $R(@LI,@I); $R(@I,*);
        $C(*,<=,@UI,@SD);
        $R(@I,@UI); $R(@UI,*);
@SD:    IF @M=3 THEN GO TO @SB;
        $R(*,@I); $R(@I,@UL);
        @LI = @LL - 1; @UI = @UL;
@SE:    IF @LI>@UI-2 THEN GO TO @SG; /* MOVE LOWER POINTER */
        @LI = @LI + 1;
        $C(@LI,<=,*,@SE);
        $R(@UI,@LI);
@SF:    @UI = @UI - 1;              /* MOVE UPPER POINTER */
```

Internal Sorting
67. A Standard Sort.
78. The Program.

```
        IF @LI>@UI-1 THEN GO TO @SG;
        $C(@UI,>,*,@SF);
        $R(@LI,@UI);
        GO TO @SE;
 @SG:   /* THE PARTITION HAS BEEN MADE; FINISH IT UP */
        IF @UI=@UL THEN DO;    /* TEST NULL UPPER SEGMENT */
          @LI = @LL - 1;
 @SH:     IF @LI>@UI-2 THEN GO TO @SJ; /* MOVE LOWER POINTER */
          @LI = @LI + 1;
          $C(@LI,<,*,@SH);
          $R(@UI,@LI);
 @SI:     @UI = @UI -1;          /* MOVE UPPER POINTER */
          IF @LI>@UI-1 THEN GO TO @SJ;
          $C(@UI,>=,*,@SI);
          $R(@LI,@UI);
          GO TO @SH;
 @SJ:     $R(@UI,*);             /* FINISH PARTITION */
          IF @UI = @LL THEN GO TO @SB; /* TEST ALL EQUAL */
          @UV(@P) = @UI - 1;
          GO TO @SA;
          END;
        /* IF UPPER SEGMENT NOT NULL, STORE BOTH SEGMENTS */
        $R(@UI,*);
        IF (@UI-@LL)<(@UL-@UI) THEN DO;
          @LV(@P+1) = @LV(@P);
          @UV(@P+1) = @UI - 1;
          @LV(@P) = @UI + 1;
 @SK:     @P = @P + 1;
          GO TO @SA;
          END;
        @LV(@P+1) = @UI + 1;
        @UV(@P+1) = @UV(@P);
        @UV(@P) = @UI - 1;
        GO TO @SK;
 @SY:   /* RETURN FROM THE PROCEDURE */

 /* TEXT BROUGHT IN BY THE INCLUDE STATEMENT ENDS HERE */

        RETURN;
        END SRT;
```

---
79. Use of the Program.

The body of the sort procedure is brought in from the library by an INCLUDE statement. The included text must be preceded by the PROCEDURE statement for the routine, the compile time procedures (par. 73), declarations of any variables to which these procedures refer, and code to set @LF and @HF to the lower and higher bounds of the segment to be sorted if these variables are not arguments of the PROCEDURE.

Internal Sorting
67. A Standard Sort.
    79. Use of the Program.

The included text must be followed by RETURN and END statements for the sort procedure. These were left out of the included
text so that if you are sorting by surrogate then you may include
the code to untangle the surrogate ahead of the RETURN statement.
    In order to specify the library where the included text is
stored, you must put the JCL card

    //P.LIB DD DSN=BCS.SOURCE.LIB,DISP=SHR

or the equivalent in the compilation step of the program deck and
then write the compile time statement

    % INCLUDE LIB(MACSORT);

at the place in the program where it is to be inserted.

----
80. Space and Timing.

    The space required for this procedure depends, of course, on
the amount of code generated by the compile-time procedures. For
the simple case illustrated, it took 2252 bytes.
    The timing for the same simple case was as follows, where

    N = file size
    T = sorting time in milliseconds
    A = $100T/(N \; LOG2(N))$.

N=	1	2	4	7	11	18	29	46	72	114
T=	.073	.101	.164	.260	.413	.721	1.22	2.07	3.51	5.90
A=	7.28	5.07	2.05	1.32	1.09	.960	.870	.814	.789	.758

N=	179	280	439	686	1073	1677	2621	4096	6400	10000
T=	9.89	16.5	27.4	45.7	75.5	124.	204.	334.	554.	899.
A=	.738	.724	.712	.706	.699	.692	.685	.680	.684	.676

----
81. Auxiliary Procedures.

    Certain procedures which are either referred to in the text
or used in the experimentation are given in this section.

----
82. Random Number Generator.

    Random numbers were obtained by the rectangular random num-
ber generator routine G2 by Miss Janet Bramhall.

```
    G2:       PROCEDURE FLOAT BINARY;
              /*  THIS FUNCTION RETURNS A RANDOM NUMBER BETWEEN
              /*  ZERO AND ONE WITH EVEN DISTRIBUTION */
          DCL I FLOAT BINARY (53) INIT(14348907) STATIC,
              J FIXED BINARY(31)   STATIC,
              Z FLOAT BIN(53) STATIC,
```

Internal Sorting
81. Auxiliary Procedures.
    82. Random Number Generator.

```
        X FLOAT BINARY (53) INIT(.3243) STATIC,
        P FLOAT BIN (53) INIT(2147483647) STATIC;
     Z=I*X;
     J=Z;
     X=Z-J + J/P;
     RETURN(X);
     END G2;
```

---

83. Timing Routines.

    Timing was done by the STIMER and TTIMER routines written by
Mr. Richard H. Potter. These are alternative entries to the
following procedure.

```
*           STIMER, TTIMER      BCC LIBRARY ROUTINE 1.07.010
*           BY DICK POTTER            JAN 1969
*
*           THESE ROUTINES PROVIDE THE PL/1 PROGRAMMER WITH
*           ACCESS TO THE STIMER AND TTIMER MACROS OF OS/360.
*
*                               SET TIMER , TEST TIMER
*           PL/I          CALL  STIMER(SEC) ;
*             TIME_REMAINING = TTIMER(0) ;
*                               N = CANCEL
*
STIMER     CSECT
           ENTRY TTIMER
           SAVE  (14,12),,*
           USING STIMER,10
           LR    10,15
           L     2,0(1)          GET  A(TIME)
           LE    0,0(2)           GET TIME
           MD    0,UNITS         CONVERT TO CPU TIMER UNITS
           AW    0,UNAC     UNORMALIZE
           STD   0,TWT           STORE
           LA    0,TTRAP          GET A(TIMER TRAP)
           LA    1,TWT+4         GET A(TIME)
           SVC   47               STIMER  SVC
           RETURN (14,12)
           EJECT
*                               RETURNS  TIME REMAINING
TTIMER     SAVE  (14,12),,*
           USING TTIMER,15
           L     10,=A(STIMER)
           DROP  15
           USING STIMER,10
           LM    2,3,0(1)
           L     1,0(2)          GET CANCEL OPTION
TTIMERX    SVC   46               TTIMER SVC
           ST    0,TWT+4         STORE CPU TIME REMAINING
           MVC   TWT(4),UNAC      SET EXPONATE
```

Internal Sorting
81. Auxiliary Procedures.
    83. Timing Routines.

```
          SDR     0,0              CLEAR REG 0
          AD      0,TWT            ADD TO NORMALIZE
          DD      0,UNITS          CONVERT TO SECONDS
          LTR     2,2              TEST FOR ONE PARAM
          BM      RTN               -  =  YES
          STE     0,0(3)           RETURN TIME
RTN       EQU     *
          RETURN (14,12)
TWT       DC      D'0'
UNITS     DC      D'38461.53846153846'   UNITS/SECOND
UNAC      DC      X'4E00000000000000'  UNORMALIZE ADD CON
*                   TIMER TRAP ENTRY
TTRAP     EQU     *
          DROP    10
          USING   TTRAP,15
          ABEND   0322,DUMP
          END
```

84. Bibliography.

This is a working bibliography on sorting methods. Entries containing the phrase 'Cited by ...' at the end have not been checked. No systematic elimination of uninteresting references has been carried out.

The following abbreviations are used:

```
CACM: Communications of the ACM
CJ:   Computer Journal
CR:   Computing Reviews
JACM: Journal of the ACM
MR:   Mathematical Reviews
```

Abrahams 1966.
P.W. Abrahams.
Review of Wierzbowski (1965).
CR 7(1966) 181 #9439.

Abrams 1965.
Philip S. Abrams.
Certification of algorithm 245: treesort 3.
CACM 8(1965) 445.
See Floyd (1964b).

Adel'son-Vel'skiy 1962.
G.M. Adel'son-Vel'skiy and Ye.M. Landis.
An algorithm for the organization of information.
Doklady Akademii Nauk SSSR, Moscow, 16,2(1962) 263-6. Translations available as U.S. Dept. of Commerce OTS JPRS 17,137; also as NASA document N63-11777.
Cited by Foster (1965a).

Alferova 1959.
Z.V. Alferova.
Methods of sorting information.
Voprosy radioelektroniki series 7 no. 2 (1959).
Cited by Pogrebinskii (1965). Not found in interlibrary search.

Applebaum 1959.
F.H. Applebaum.
Variable word sorting in the RCA 501 system.
Paper 44, Preprints, 14th Nat. Meeting ACM, Cambridge, Mass., 3 pp.
Uses a variable-way internal merge followed by external N-way merges, reading backward on alternate passes.

Internal Sorting
84. Bibliography.

Arora 1969.
    S.R. Arora and W.T. Dent.
    Randomized binary search technique.
    CACM 12(1969)77-80.
    Mathematical model for mean and variance of number of com-
        parisons required to search a binary tree. Reviewed by
        Gold (1969).

Ashenhurst 1953.
    R.L. Ashenhurst.
    Sorting and arranging.
    Harvard Comput. Lab., Rep. No. BL-7, Theory of Switching,
        Sect. 1. 1953.
    Cited by Bayes (1968).

Baer 1962.
    Robert M. Baer and Paul Brock.
    Natural Sorting.
    SIAM J. 10(1962)284-304.
    Investigates the distribution function of the lengths of
        ordered subsequences of a random sequence.

Barrett 1958.
    M. Barrett.
    Letter.
    CJ 1(1958)123.
    The argument for base 2 in Bell (1958) is incorrect and
        probably irrelevant.

Batcher 1964a.
    K.E. Batcher.
    A new internal sorting method.
    Goodyear Aerospace Report GER-11759, 1964.
    Cited by Batcher (1968).

Batcher 1964b.
    K.E. Batcher.
    Bitonic sorting.
    Goodyear Aerospace Report GER-11869, 1964.
    Cited by Batcher (1968).

Batcher 1968.
    K.E. Batcher.
    Sorting networks and their applications.
    AFIPS Conference Proceedings vol. 32: 1968 Spring Joint
        Computer Conference. Thompson Book Co., Washington,
        1968, pp. 307-14.
    A special digital comparison circuit has two inputs and two
        outputs; one output is the smaller of the two inputs
        and the other is the larger. A logical device construc-
        ted of such circuits could sort rapidly.

Internal Sorting
84. Bibliography.

Batty 1964.
    M.A. Batty.
    Certification of algorithm 201: Shellsort.
    CACM 7(1964)349.
    See Boothroyd (1963).

Bayer 1970.
    R. Bayer and E. McCreight.
    Organization and maintenance of large ordered indices.
    Boeing Scientific Research Laboratories, Mathematical and
        Information Sciences Report No. 20, July 1970. 33 pp.
        AD 712079.
    A large index file is maintained on random access storage as
        a B-tree: the root may have from 1 to 2k+1 sons; every
        other non-leaf has from k+1 to 2k+1 sons; each terminal
        node is at the same height. Insertion, deletion and
        retrieval algorithms are described. The optimum value
        of k is determined.

Bayes 1968.
    A. Bayes.
    A generalized partial pass block sort.
    CACM 11(1968)491-3.
    A radix sort to tape, most significant digit first, with
        final internal sort.

Bell 1958.
    D.A. Bell.
    The principles of sorting.
    CJ 1(Jul 1958)71-77.
    The search for general principles is not very successful.
        The pigeon-hole, radix, merging, repeated comparison,
        insertion, address calculation, selection, and counting
        methods are evaluated. For comments, see Barrett
        (1958), Venn (1958), Fairthorne (1959).

Belzer 1964.
    Jack Belzer.
    Review of Goetz (1964).
    CR 5(1964)316-7 #6402.

Berners Lee 1960.
    C.M. Berners Lee.
    Letters.
    CJ 3(1960)174,184.
    The tree sorting method attributed to Berners Lee by Windley
        (1960) is here attributed to D.J. Wheeler (no refer-
        ence). On the Pegasus computer it takes less space and
        more time than merging.

Internal Sorting
84. Bibliography.

Betz 1959.
    B.K. Betz and W.C. Carter.
    New merge sorting techniques.
    Preprint 14, 14th Nat. ACM meeting, Cambridge, 1959. 4 pp.
    Uses n-1 initial data tapes and one blank; (n-1)-way merges
        until one tape is empty, then (n-2)-way until the next
        tape is empty, etc. If initial tapes have the right
        number of strings, the method self-perpetuates.

Beus 1967.
    H. Lynn Beus.
    The use of information in sorting.
    Case Western Reserve U., Computing Center Rep. No. 1096,
        Ph.D. thesis, 1967.
    Cited by Beus (1970).

Beus 1970.
    H. Lynn Beus.
    The use of information in sorting.
    JACM 17(1970)482-95.
    The 'information' used is that resulting from transitivity,
        as applied to sequences of comparisons.

Beyer 1967.
    G. Beyer.
    Review of Gassner (1967).
    CR 8(1967)287 #12091.

Black 1970.
    Neville A. Black.
    Optimum merging from mass storage.
    CACM 13(1970)745-9.
    Gives an algorithm which yields the orders of successive
        merge passes such that total read time is minimized.

Blair 1964.
    Charles R. Blair.
    Certification of algorithm 207: stringsort.
    CACM 7(1964)585.
    See Boothroyd (1963b).

Blair 1966.
    Charles R. Blair.
    Certification of algorithm 271: quickersort.
    CACM 9(1966)354.
    Gives timing for several algorithms (201,207,245,271) on CDC
        1604A. 271 is substantially fastest.

Internal Sorting
84. Bibliography.

Blum 1954.
    Blum and Fogg.
    Sorting on the 701.
    Proc. IBM Computing Seminar. May 1954.
    Cited by Hosken (1955). Not available from IBM.

Boehm 1957.
    Carl Boehm.
    Die Bereinigung eines Versicherungsbestandes als Sonderfall
        des Mischprozesses (The updating of an insurance policy
        file as a special case of the merging process).
    Deutsche Gesellschaft fuer Versicherungsmathematik (Deutsch-
        er Aktuarverein) e.v. Koeln/Rhein 3,3(1957)323-52.
    Detailed discussion of the two-way merge, with flow charts
        and sample program.

Boehm 1961a.
    Carl Boehm.
    Sortierprozesse auf elektronischen Rechenanlagen (Sorting on
        electronic computers).
    Blaetter der Deutsche Gesellschaft fuer Versicherungsmathe-
        matik (Deutscher Aktuarverein) e.v. Koeln/Rhein 5,2(Apr
        1961)155-205.
    Gives description, flowchart, and time/space calculations
        for ten internal sorting methods. 38 references.

Boehm 1961b.
    C. Boehm.
    Die Zahl der Vergleichsoperationen beim Mischen auf drei
        Bahnen (The number of comparisons in merging from three
        tapes).
    Mitt. Verein. Schweiz. Versich.-Math. 61(1961)65-75.
    Derives formula for the number of comparisons needed.

Boothroyd 1963.
    J. Boothroyd.
    Algorithm 201: Shellsort.
    CACM 6(1963)445.
    See Chandler (1970), Batty (1964).

Boothroyd 1963b.
    J. Boothroyd.
    Algorithm 207: stringsort.
    CACM 6(1963)615.
    Certified by Blair (1964).

Internal Sorting
84. Bibliography.

Boothroyd 1967.
    J. Boothroyd.
    Algorithm 25: sort a section of the elements of an array by
        determining the rank of each element (partsort).
    Algorithm 26: Order the subscripts of an array section
        according to the magnitudes of the elements (keysort).
    Algorithm 27: Rearrange the elements of an array section
        according to a permutation of the subscripts (permvec-
        tor).
    CJ 10(1967/8)308-10.
    Gives an improved Algol version of Quickersort (Scowen
        1965).

Bose 1961.
    R.C. Bose and R.J. Nelson.
    A sorting problem.
    Math. Sciences Directorate, Air Force Office Scientific
        Res., Washington, Apr 1961, 22pp.
    Reviewed by Harling (1961).

Bose 1962.
    R.C. Bose and R.J. Nelson.
    A sorting problem.
    JACM 9(1962)282-96.
    The method of this paper is discussed in par. 47. Reviewed
        by Floyd (1962b).

Brawn 1969.
    B. Brawn, F. Gustavson and E. Mankin.
    Sorting performance in a paged virtual memory.
    IBM, T.J. Watson Research Center, Yorktown Heights, RC-2435,
        Apr 1969.
    Gives experimental results for various internal sorting
        methods: Quicksort, merge, and combination of the two;
        direct and by surrogate. Considers other methods and
        discusses principles leading to minimal paging excep-
        tions.

Brawn 1970.
    Barbara S. Brawn, Frances G. Gustavson and Efrem S. Mankin.
    Sorting in a paging environment.
    CACM 13(1970)483-94.

Bridges 1954.
    D.B.J. Bridges et al.
    Preliminary systems design and operational analysis for the
        MIFD (Material Information-Flow Device).
    WADC Tech. Rep. 53-505, Wright-Patterson AFB, 1954.
    Cited by Teichrow (1963).

Brock, Paul: See Baer (1962)

Internal Sorting
84. Bibliography.

Brock 1959.
    Paul Brock.
    Problem 59-3: Optimum sorting procedure.
    SIAM Rev. 1(1959)70-1.
    A lemma concerning maximal nondecreasing subsequences in a
        random binary sequence. Solution by Brock in SIAM Rev.
        2(1960)155-6.

Brock 1960.
    Paul Brock.
    Problem 60-2: On a binomial identity arising from a sorting
        problem.
    SIAM Rev. 2(1960)40.

Buhagiar 1968.
    Jan Buhagiar and Alan Jons.
    A scan sort using two tape units.
    Computer Bulletin (May 1968)11-12.
    The input tape is repeatedly scanned. At each scan, a work-
        ing area is filled with the n lowest records not yet
        selected. At the end of the scan these n records are
        sorted internally and put on the output tape. Reviewed
        by Hamilton (1968).

Burge 1958.
    W.H. Burge.
    Sorting, trees and measures of order.
    Information and Control 1(1958)181-97.
    Optimal strategies for merging and distribution sorting are
        related to tree structures in various ways.

Burge 1965.
    W.H. Burge.
    Review of Glicksman (1965).
    CR 6(1965)348 #8341.

Burroughs 1961a.
    Burroughs Corporation.
    Sorting on the B5000.
    Bull. 5000-21004 Sept 1961.
    Cited by Teichrow (1963).

Burroughs 1961b.
    Burroughs Corporation.
    A sort generator program for the Burroughs 200 computer.
    Tech. Bull. TB-117. Rev. 19 July 1961.
    Cited by Teichrow (1963).

Internal Sorting
84. Bibliography.

Burroughs 1963.
    Burroughs Corporation.
    Preliminary information on magnetic tape sort generator I
        for the B270 and B280 systems.
    Bull. 200-21005, Mar. 1963.
    Cited by Teichrow (1963). Not available from Burroughs.

Canning 1957.
    Richard G. Canning.
    How the four-tape sorter simplifies storage.
    Control Engineering 4,4(Feb 1957)95-7.
    Three manufacturers supply off-line electronic sorters to
        carry out a 2x2 merge of magnetic tapes.

Carlitz 1964.
    L. Carlitz.
    A binomial identity arising from a sorting problem.
    SIAM Rev. 6(1964)20-30.
    Proof for Brock (1960) identity.

Carter, W.C.: See Betz (1959)

Carter 1962.
    W.C. Carter.
    Mathematical analysis of merge-sorting techniques.
    Proceedings of IFIP Congress 1962. North-Holland Pub. Co.,
        Amsterdam, 1963, pp. 62-5.
    Balanced, cascade, and polyphase tape merging methods are
        analysed using difference equations.

Carter 1963.
    W.C. Carter.
    Review of Mendoza (1962).
    CR 4(1963)81 #3866.

CDC 1962.
    Control Data Corporation.
    Sort 3X.
    Nov. 1962.
    Cited by Teichrow (1963).

CDC 1963.
    Control Data Corporation.
    Control Data 1604 generalized sort program.
    Jan 1963.
    Cited by Teichrow (1963).

Internal Sorting
84. Bibliography.

CDC 1966.
Control Data Corporation.
Computer systems mass storage sort.
CDC No. 60174100, Sep. 1966.
The internal sort is by replacement selection using the tournament method.

CDC 1968.
Control Data Corporation.
Computer systems tape sort merge.
CDC No. 60227900, Mar. 1968.
The internal sort is the same as in CDC (1966).

Chandler 1970.
J.P. Chandler and W.C. Harrison.
Remark on Algorithm 201: Shellsort.
CACM 13(1970)373-4.
Timing comparisons for Shell sort (Boothroyd 1963) with and without the improvement suggested by Hibbard (1963), on CDC 6400, using Algol, Fortran, and Compass.

Chestermann 1959.
J.F. Chestermann.
Sorting methods in large business operations.
Bell Lab. Rec. (1959)337-41.
Describes straight pxp tape merge with (unspecified) internal sort.

Cheydleur 1965.
B.F. Cheydleur, R. Kronmal and M. Tarter.
Cumulative polygon address sorting.
Proc. ACM 20th Natl. Conf., Cleveland, Aug 1965, pp. 376-85.
Reviewed by Goldstine (1966).

Clampett 1964.
Harry A. Clampett, Jr.
Randomized binary searching with tree structures.
CACM 7(1964)163-5.

Clapp 1959.
David F. Clapp.
A survey of sorting.
Massachusetts Institute of Technology, Lincoln Laboratory, Memo No. 2M-0356, 7 May 1959. 36pp.
Discusses merging, distributing (radix), selecting, counting, exchanging (transposition), and inserting (ranking) sorting methods, with flow charts. References.

Internal Sorting
84. Bibliography.

Cline 1955.
 R.L. Cline.
 Sorting and merging on electronic data processing machines.
 ACM meeting 1955.
 Cited by Hosken (1955). Not found in interlibrary search.

Cooke 1963.
 William S. Cooke.
 A tape file merge pattern generator.
 CACM 6(1963)227-30.
 Computer program specifies schema of merge cycles.

Cox 1956.
 B. Cox and J. Goldberg.
 A magnetic-drum sorting system.
 IRE Nat. Conv. Rec. 4(1956)101-4.
 A special magnetic drum sorter is used for incoming transac-
   tions in the ERMA computer.

Davies 1956.
 D.W. Davies.
 Sorting of data on an electronic computer.
 Proc. Inst. Elect. Engrs. 103B (1956) Supplement 1 p. 87-93.
 Mainly concerned with magnetic tape sorting.

de Beauclair 1961.
 W. De Beauclair.
 Das Sortieren von Magnetband-Daten in einfachen Buchungsan-
   lagen.
 Elektr. Rechen. 2(Apr 1961)75-81.
 Reviewed by Hamblen (1962). Review of tape sorting, with
   emphasis on modifications of the ascending decimal
   radix sort to reduce the number of tapes needed.

DeFiore 1970.
 Casper R. DeFiore.
 Fast sorting.
 Datamation (1 Aug 1970)47-51.
 Use of Goodyear associative memory with CDC 1604B computer
   provides fast sorting. See letters, Datamation 1 Oct
   1970 p. 9.

de la Briandais 1959.
 Rene de la Briandais.
 File searching using variable length keys.
 Proc. Western Joint Comp. Conf. 1959. p. 295-8.
 Stores a list of words as a tree. Counting the root as level
   zero, each first letter of a word is a node at level
   one. Each second letter that occurs after a given first
   letter is a node filial to the node for that first
   letter, and so on.

Internal Sorting
84. Bibliography.

Demuth 1956.
      Howard B. Demuth.
      A report on electronic data sorting.
      Stanford Research Institute Report No. 52410-2, Oct 1956.
      Investigates sorting using abstractions of drum, tape, and
            core memories. Finds lower bound log(n!) for number of
            comparisons.

Demuth 1957.
      Howard B. Demuth.
      Sorting on electronic digital computers.
      Stanford U., Ph.D. thesis, 1957.
      Cited by Beus (1970).

Denning 1968.
      P.J. Denning.
      Review of Foster (1968).
      CR 9(1968)735 #15786.

Dent, W.T.: See Arora (1969)

Dinsmore 1965.
      R.J. Dinsmore.
      Longer strings from sorting.
      CACM 8(1965)48.
      Replacement selection gives longer strings for first merge
            pass.

Douglas 1958.
      A.S. Douglas.
      Computers and commerce.
      CJ 1(1958)132.
      Cited by Douglas (1959).

Douglas 1959.
      A.S. Douglas.
      Techniques for the recording of, and reference to data in a
            computer.
      CJ 2(1959)1-9.
      General discussion of the storing of and reference to
            labeled data in a computer. Several sorting methods are
            described.

Fairthorne 1959.
      R.A. Fairthorne.
      Letter.
      CJ 1(1959)171.
      Attacks the choice of 2 as selection base in Bell (1958).

Internal Sorting
84. Bibliography.

Falkin 1963.
     Joel Falkin and Sal Savastano, Jr.
     Sorting with large volume, random access, drum storage.
     CACM 6(1963)240-4.

Feerst 1959.
     S. Feerst and F. Sherwood.
     The effect of simultaneity of sorting operations.
     Preprint 42, 14th Nat. ACM meeting, Cambridge, 1959. 3 pp.

Ferguson 1971.
     David E. Ferguson.
     Buffer allocation in merge-sorting.
     CACM 14(1971)476-8.
     Allocating input buffers proportional to the square roots of
          the string lengths in a merge pass reduces the number
          of disk seeks.

Feurzeig 1960.
     Wallace Feurzeig.
     Algorithm 23: mathsort.
     CACM 3(1960)600-1.
     An address calculation sort for numbers. Certified by Ran-
          shaw (1961).

Flies 1969.
     William P. Flies and Thomas L. Yates.
     Sorting: make technique fit the job.
     Data Management (Dec 1969)34-6.
     Brief and nontechnical review of techniques and criteria.

Flores 1960.
     Ivan Flores.
     Computing time for address calculation sorting.
     JACM 7(1960)389-409.
     Gives flowchart, timing formulas, and test data. Reviewed by
          Rechard (1961).

Flores 1961.
     Ivan Flores.
     Analysis of internal computer sorting.
     JACM 8(1961)41-80.
     Gives description, flow chart and timing formulas for all
          internal sorting methods known to the author at that
          time: insertion, counting, exchanging, radix, selec-
          tion, merging, address calculation. Algorithms given in
          Flores (1962).

Internal Sorting
84. Bibliography.

Flores 1962.
       I. Flores.
       Algorithm 76: sorting procedures.
       CACM 5(1962)48-50.
       These are the procedures discussed in Flores (1961). See
              Randell (1962).

Flores 1969.
       I. Flores.
       Computer sorting.
       Prentice-Hall, Englewood Cliffs, N.J., 1969.
       Develops a special notation for describing sorting methods,
              and gives programming examples. Internal sorting
              discussion not up to date. Reviewed by Yarbrough
              (1969).

Floyd 1962.
       Robert W. Floyd.
       Algorithm 113: treesort.
       CACM 5(1962)434.
       Cf. Kaupe (1962).

Floyd 1962b.
       Robert W. Floyd.
       Review of Bose (1962).
       CR 3(1962)207 #2620.

Floyd 1964.
       Robert W. Floyd.
       Algorithm 245: Treesort 3.
       CACM 7(1964)701.
       Certified by London (1970), Abrams (1965). See par. 65 for
              discussion.

Fogg: See Blum (1954)

Foster 1965a.
       C.C. Foster.
       Information storage and retrieval using AVL trees.
       Proc. ACM 20th National Conference, Cleveland, August, 1965,
              pp. 192-205.
       The length of a subtree is the number of nodes in the
              longest path within that subtree. An AVL tree is a
              binary tree such that, for every node, the lengths of
              the two subtrees dependent from that node differ by at
              most 1. This structure is due to Adel'son-Vel'skiy
              (1962). The number of operations required to manage
              such a tree is estimated.

Internal Sorting
84. Bibliography.

Foster 1965b.
    C.C. Foster.
    A study of AVL trees.
    Goodyear Aerospace Corp. Akron, 1965, GER-12158.
    Cited by Foster (1965a).

Foster 1968.
    Caxton C. Foster.
    Sorting almost ordered arrays.
    CJ 11(1968)134-7.
    The N segments of the array that are already in sort are
        combined in an N-way merge. Reviewed by Denning (1968).

Fox 1966.
    D. Fox.
    Review of MacLaren (1966).
    CR 7(1966)521 #10873.

Frank 1960.
    R.M. Frank and R.B. Lazarus.
    A high-speed sorting procedure.
    CACM 3(1960)20-22.
    An analysis of the Shell sort shows that odd values of m
        should be chosen.

Frazer 1969.
    W.D. Frazer and A.C. McKellar.
    Samplesort: a sampling approach to minimal storage time
        sorting.
    In Proc. Third Annual Princeton Conf. on Information Scien-
        ces and Systems, 1969, pp. 276-80.
    This method is discussed in par. 58.

Frazer 1970.
    W.D. Frazer and A.C. McKellar.
    Samplesort: a sampling approach to minimal storage tree
        sorting.
    JACM 17(1970)496-507.
    This procedure uses Hoare's Quicksort, except that a large
        sample is first sorted and then used to provide estima-
        ted medians for successive segments.

Fredkin 1960.
    E. Fredkin.
    Trie memory.
    CACM 3(1960)490-9.
    A trie is a radix tree with one level of nodes for each
        digit.

Internal Sorting
84. Bibliography.

French 1963.
      Norman C. French.
      Computer planned collates.
      CACM 6(1963)225-7.
      Computer finds optimal schema for merging multiple files.

Friend 1956.
      Edward Harry Friend.
      Sorting on electronic computer systems.
      JACM 3(1956)134-68.
      General discussion of sorting magnetic tape files. Internal
            methods include merging, inserting, exchanging, count-
            ing, selecting, replacement selecting, and radix.

Friend 1960.
      E.H. Friend.
      Sorting on electronic computer systems.
      South African Computer Bulletin 2(Nov 1960).
      Cited by CR 2(1961)148 #1068. This journal not located by
            interlibrary search.

Gale 1970.
      David Gale and Richard M. Karp.
      A phenomenon in the theory of sorting.
      IEEE Conference Record of 1970 Eleventh Annual Symposium on
            Switching and Automata Theory. 28-30 October 1970, pp.
            51-9.
      Investigates the conditions under which a partial sort
            remains undisturbed by another partial sorting opera-
            tion.

Gassner 1967.
      Betty Jane Gassner.
      Sorting by replacement selecting.
      CACM 10(1967)89-93.
      Gives expected string lengths to first merge pass. Reviewed
            by Beyer (1967).

GE 1962.
      General Electric Company.
      GE-225 forward sort-merge generator.
      Jul 1962.
      Cited by Teichrow (1963).

Gear 1966.
      C.W. Gear.
      Review of Svoboda (1963).
      CR 7(1966)327 #10086.

Internal Sorting
84. Bibliography.

Gilstad 1960.
    R.L. Gilstad.
    Polyphase merge sorting - an advanced technique.
    Proc. Eastern Joint Comp. Conf. 1960. p. 143-8.

Gilstad 1963.
    R.L. Gilstad.
    Read-backward polyphase sorting.
    CACM 6(1963)220-3.

Gladun 1965.
    V.P. Gladun and Z.L. Rabinovich.
    Fast sorting methods in the internal memory.
    Cybernetics 1,1(Jan-Feb 1965)94-101; English translation
        from Kibernetika 1,1(1965)92-99.
    Two algorithms based on radix sorting via an auxiliary
        matrix are described.

Gladun 1965b.
    V.P. Gladun.
    Storage organization for key search and recording.
    Cybernetics 1,4(Aug 1965).
    Cited by Bayer (1970).

Glicksman 1965.
    Stephen Glicksman.
    Concerning the merging of equal length tape files.
    JACM 12(1965)254-8.
    A procedure for merging k equal-length tape files by at most
        r-way merges minimizes tape reading and writing times
        when b of the files are merged n-1 times and k-b are
        merged n times; b and n are derived. Reviewed by Burge
        (1965).

Glore 1963.
    John B. Glore.
    Sorting nonredundant files - techniques used in the FACT
        compiler.
    CACM 6(1963)231-40.

Goetz 1963.
    Martin A. Goetz.
    Internal and tape sorting using the replacement-selection
        technique.
    CACM 6(1963)201-6.
    Shows that if there is room for N records in storage, the
        initial strings will average 2N records, and that 1 +
        $\log_2(N)$ tests per record are required. The method can
        be used internally, at the cost of N additional poin-
        ter-cells and N exchanges.

Internal Sorting
84. Bibliography.

Goetz 1963b.
    Martin A. Goetz and Gloria S. Toth.
    A comparison between the polyphase and oscillating sort
        techniques.
    CACM 6(1963) 223-5.
    Polyphase superior with fewer than 8 tapes, oscillating
        better with more than 8.

Goetz 1963c.
    Martin A. Goetz.
    Organization and structure of data on disk file memory
        systems for efficient sorting and other data processing
        programs.
    CACM 6(1963) 245-8.

Goetz 1963d.
    Martin A. Goetz.
    Design and characteristics of a variable-length record sort
        using new fixed-length record sorting techniques.
    CACM 6(1963) 264-7.

Goetz 1963e.
    Martin A. Goetz.
    Letter.
    CACM 6(1963) 585-6.
    Exchange with Knuth on cascade and polyphase merges.

Goetz 1964.
    Martin A. Goetz.
    Some improvements in the technology of string merging and
        internal sorting.
    AFIPS Conf. Proc. vol. 25, 1964 Spring Joint Comp. Conf.,
        pp. 599-607.
    Oscillating merge for read-forward tapes. Reviewed by Belzer
        (1964).

Gold 1969.
    D.E. Gold.
    Review of Arora (1969).
    CR 10(1969) 326-7 #17052.

Goldberg, J.: See Cox (1956)

Goldenberg 1952.
    D. Goldenberg.
    Time analysis of various methods of sorting data.
    MIT Digital Computing Lab. Div. 6, Memo M1680 (17 Oct 1952).
    Cited by Teichrow (1963).

Internal Sorting
84. Bibliography.

Goldstine 1948.
     Herman H. Goldstine and John von Neumannn.
     Planning and coding of problems for an electronic computing
          instrument. Volume 2 of Part II.
     Princeton University Press, April 1948, 68 pp. Reprinted in
          the Collected Works of John von Neumann, vol. V:
          "Design of Computers, Theory of Automata and Numerical
          Analysis", Pergamon Press, Oxford, 1963; Macmillan Co.,
          New York, 1963; pp. 152-214.
     Chapter 11, "Coding of some Combinatorial (Sorting) Prob-
          lems", pp. 196-214, displays the code for meshing
          (= 2-way merge) and a straight binary merge sort (par.
          25 of the present book).

Goldstine 1966.
     H.H. Goldstine.
     Review of Cheydleur (1965).
     CR 7(1966)163 #9333.

Gotlieb 1960.
     C.C. Gotlieb.
     Review of Hildebrandt (1959).
     CACM 3(1960)283.

Gotlieb 1960b.
     C.C. Gotlieb.
     Review of Hildebrandt (1959).
     CR 1(1960)9 #21.

Gotlieb 1961.
     C.C. Gotlieb.
     Review of Windley (1959).
     CR 2(1961)12 #476, also MR 21(1960) #4574.

Gotlieb 1963.
     C.C. Gotlieb.
     Sorting on computers.
     CACM 6(1963)194-201. Reprinted from "Applications of Digital
          Computers", Ginn and Co., Boston, 1963.
     General review of internal sorting, tape sorting, and sort
          generators.

Graham 1960.
     J.W. Graham.
     Data sorting with digital computers.
     Proc. Second Conf., Computing and Data Processing Society of
          Canada, p. 211-25.
     Mainly concerned with magnetic tape sorting.

Internal Sorting
84. Bibliography.

Grandage 1966.
    A. Grandage.
    Review of Picard (1966).
    CR 7 (1966) 437 #10572.

Grau 1961.
    Albert A. Grau.
    Review of Nagler (1960).
    CR 2 (1961) 82 #809.

Graves 1968.
    R.L. Graves.
    Review of Outrata (1966).
    CR 9 (1968) 552 #15207.

Gray, H.J.: See Prywes (1962)

Griffin 1970.
    Robin Griffin and K.A. Reddish.
    Remark on algorithm 347.
    CACM 13 (1970) 54.
    Verifies this algorithm (Singleton 1969), suggests minor
        changes, gives timing results for CDC 6400, IBM 7040.

Grisoff 1963.
    Stephen Grisoff.
    Review of Lautz (1963).
    CR 4 (1963) 266 #4718-9.

Guerber 1960.
    Howard P. Guerber.
    Sorting apparatus.
    U.S. Patent 2,935,732 filed 3 May 1954 granted 3 May 1960.
        Assigned to Radio Corporation of America.
    Describes a special purpose device for a straight two-by-two
        tape merge sort.

Gustavson, Frances G.: See Brawn (1969), Brawn (1970).

Hall 1963.
    Michael H. Hall.
    A method of comparing the time requirements of sorting
        methods.
    CACM 6 (1963) 259-63.

Hamblen 1962.
    John W. Hamblen.
    Review of de Beauclair (1961).
    CR 3 (1962) 187 #2405.

Internal Sorting
84. Bibliography.

Hamilton 1968.
    D.E. Hamilton.
    Review of Buhagiar (1968).
    CR 9(1968)552 #15208.

Harel 1967.
    A. Harel.
    Review of Yuval (1967).
    CR 8(1967)353 #12357.

Harling 1961.
    R.T. Harling.
    Review of Bose (1961).
    CR 2(1961)203 #1275.

Harrison, W.C.: See Chandler (1970)

Hayes 1958.
    R.M. Hayes.
    Magnacard sorting techniques.
    13th National ACM Meeting, Urbana, Jun 1958, preprint 48.
    Combined use of central processor and the Magnacard Handling
        Unit, which processes 1x3 inch strips of magnetic tape,
        speeds merge-sorting.

Hendrix 1963.
    V.L. Hendrix.
    Review of Schick (1963).
    CR 6(1963)283-4 #4806.

Hibbard 1962a.
    Thomas N. Hibbard.
    Some combinatorial properties of certain trees, with appli-
        cations to searching and sorting.
    JACM 9(1962)13-28.
    Analyzes the binary search tree as a data structure that can
        be searched efficiently and also changed efficiently.
        Gives an empirical estimate for number of comparisons
        for Shell's method.

Hibbard 1962b.
    Thomas N. Hibbard.
    A simple sorting algorithm.
    System Development Corp. TM-718/000/01, Aug 1962
    Cited by Hibbard (1963).

Internal Sorting
84. Bibliography.

Hibbard 1963.
    Thomas N. Hibbard.
    An empirical study of minimal storage sorting.
    CACM 6(1963)206-13.
    Four programs were tested: A) radix exchange; B) binary
        partition; C) Shell sort; D) like Shell, but on dis-
        joint sequences. Three types of random files were used.
        Algol programs and experimental results (IBM 709/7090)
        are given.

Hibbard 1963b.
    Thomas N. Hibbard.
    A simple sorting algorithm.
    JACM 10(1963)142-50.
    This algorithm is based on Bose (1962) and requires the same
        number of comparisons. Reviewed by van der Poel (1964).
        See par. 49.

Hildebrandt 1959.
    P. Hildebrandt and H. Isbitz.
    Radix exchange: an internal sorting method for digital com-
        puters.
    JACM 6(1959)156-63.
    This is apparently the first publication of binary radix
        sort, most significant bit first. Reviewed (Gotlieb
        1960, 1960b).

Hillmore 1962.
    J.S. Hillmore.
    Certification of algorithms 63, 64, 65: Partition, Quick-
        sort, Find.
    CACM 5(1962)439.
    See Hoare (1961).

Hoare 1961.
    C.A.R. Hoare.
    Algorithm 64: Quicksort.
    CACM 4(1961)321.
    Certified by Hillmore (1962), Randell (1963).

Hoare 1962.
    C.A.R. Hoare.
    Quicksort.
    CJ 5(1962)10-15.
    The method of this paper is discussed in par. 55.

Internal Sorting
84. Bibliography.

Hoare 1971.
    C.A.R. Hoare.
    Proof of a program: FIND.
    CACM 14(1971)39-45.
    Given an array A(1:N) and a number $1 \leq f \leq N$, the program per-
        mutes A so that if $1 \leq i \leq f \leq j \leq N$ then $A(i) \leq A(f)$ and $A(f) \leq$
        $A(j)$. Note the resemblance to a Quicksort partition
        (par. 55). The main feature of the paper is a logical
        proof of correctness of FIND, and the references are
        relevant to proving correctness.

Holberton 1954.
    F.E. Holberton.
    Sorting rerun procedure, incorporated in the master generat-
        ing routine; two-way sorting.
    Univac Memo 100 (1954).
    Cited by Hosken (1955).

Holzmann, H.J.: See Lytton (1956)

Honeywell 1961a.
    Minneapolis-Honeywell Regulator Company.
    ARGUS sort and collate manual.
    DSI-43A/2562, 1961.
    Cited by Teichrow (1963).

Honeywell 1962a.
    Minneapolis-Honeywell Regulator Company.
    EASY I: sort and collate routines for the Honeywell 400.
    Bulletin No. 102, DSI-131-9462, 1962.
    Cited by Teichrow (1963).

Honeywell 1962b.
    Minneapolis-Honeywell Regulator Company.
    EASY II: sort and collate routines for the HONEYWELL 400.
    Bulletin No. 103, DSI 132-91762, 1962.
    Cited by Teichrow (1963).

Hooker 1969.
    William W. Hooker.
    On the expected lengths of sequences generated in sorting by
        replacement selecting.
    CACM 12(1969)411-3.

Hosken 1955.
    J.C. Hosken.
    Evaluation of sorting methods.
    Proc. Eastern Joint Computer Conf. 1955, pp. 39-55.
    This paper deals mainly with special mechanisms used for
        sorting, but references are made to early computer
        methods as well.

Internal Sorting
84. Bibliography.

Howard 1956.
P.H. Howard.
Comparison of sorting methods.
IBM 705 Memo 80, 10.
Cited by Teichrow (1963). Not available from IBM.

Hubbard 1963.
George U. Hubbard.
Some characteristics of sorting in computing systems using
random access storage devices.
CACM 6(1963) 248-55.
Considers optimum order of merge.

Hurwitz 1971.
H. Hurwitz Jr.
On the probability distribution of the values of binary
trees.
CACM 14(1971)99-102.
An integral equation is given for the generating function
for binary tree values, which are related to sorting
effort for the Quicksort family of sorting algorithms.
The first three resulting moments are compared with
previcus results and empirical data.

IBM 0000a.
International Business Machines Corporation.
Sorting methods for IBM data processing systems.
J28-8001.
Cited by Lombardi (1962). Not available from IBM.

IBM 0000b.
International Business Machines Corporation.
Sorting techniques.
C20-1639.
Cited by Bayes (1968). Out of print; no replacement.

IBM 1955.
International Business Machines Corporation.
702 sorting techniques; two-way merge.
EDPM program brief 8, form 22-6656-0, 1955.
Cited by Hosken (1955). Not available from IBM.

IBM 1957a.
International Business Machines Corporation.
705 generalized merge program. Merge 52.
32-7626, 1957.
Cited by Teichrow (1963). Not available from IBM.

Internal Sorting
84. Bibliography.

IBM 1957b.
     International Business Machines Corporation.
     705 generalized sorting program. Sort 53A.
     32-6968-1, 1957.
     Cited by Teichrow (1963). Not available from IBM.

IBM 1958a.
     International Business Machines Corporation.
     Sorting methods for IBM data processing systems (650, 704,
          709, and 705).
     F28-8001, 1958.
     Cited by Teichrow (1963). Not available from IBM.

IBM 1959a.
     International Business Machines Corporation.
     Sort III, IBM 650 tape sorting program.
     C28-4022, 1959.
     Cited by Teichrow (1963). Not available from IBM.

IBM 1959b.
     International Business Machines Corporation.
     Sort 7090 timing tables.
     J28-6043, Share distribution 607, 1959.
     Cited by Teichrow (1963). Not available from IBM.

IBM 1961a.
     International Business Machines Corporation.
     IBM 7070/7074 Generalized sorting program. Sort 90.
     C28-6111, 1961.
     Method used for internal sorting is not discussed.

Isaac 1956.
     E.J. Isaac and R.C. Singleton.
     Sorting by address calculation.
     JACM 3(1956) 169-74.
     This paper, presented in Sep 1955, may be the first on the
          subject. Each item is stored in an address calculated
          from its key, with conflicts resolved by actual key
          comparisons.

Isbitz, H.: See Hildebrandt (1959)

Isenburg 1940.
     Wilhem Karl Prinz von Isenburg.
     Historische Genealogie.
     Verlag von R. Oldenbourg, Munich and Berlin, 1940, 101pp.
     Attributes vector numbering of binary trees to Michael
          Eizinger in 1590.

Internal Sorting
84. Bibliography.

Iverson 1962.
      Kenneth E. Iverson.
      A programming language.
      John Wiley and Sons, New York, 1962. xxi+286.
      Chapter 6 of this general introduction to APL deals with
            sorting. For the sorting method used by APL, see
            Woodrum (1969).

Johnson 1958.
      L.R. Johnson and R.D. Pratt.
      An introduction to the complete UNIVAC II sort-merge system
            SESAME.
      Univac Rev. (Fall 1958).
      Cited by Teichrow (1963). Mrs. Alma B. Campbell, Librarian
            of Univac Data Processing Division, Blue Bell, Pa.
            19422, very kindly attempted to locate this copy of the
            Review, but without success. She provided the reference
            (Johnson 1959) on the same topic.

Johnson 1959.
      Lyle R. Johnson and Richard D. Pratt.
      SESAME opens the door to programming simplification.
      UNIVAC Review (Winter 1959) 13-17.
      SESAME (SErvice Sort And MErge) is a general purpose sort-
            merge package for UNIVAC II, using replacement-selec-
            tion for the internal sort.

Johnson 1970.
      Lyle R. Johnson.
      System structure in data, programs, and computers.
      Prentice-Hall, Inc., Englewood Cliffs, N.J., 1970. xiii +
            303 pp.
      Chapters 3 "Table Searching" and 4 "Table Sorting" are a
            propos.

Jones,B. 1970.
      Bush Jones.
      A variation on sorting by address calculation.
      CACM 13(1970) 105-7.
      Uses a combination of address calculation and merging.

Jons, Alan: See Buhagiar (1968)

Juelich 1963.
      O.C. Juelich.
      Remark on algorithm 175: shuttle sort.
      CACM 6(1963) 739.
      Criticizes Shaw (1963), retracts in Juelich (1964).

Internal Sorting
84. Bibliography.

Juelich 1964.
    O.C. Juelich.
    Remark on algorithm 175: shuttle sort.
    CACM 7(1964)296.
    Juelich (1963) incorrect in saying Shaw (1963) contained
        errors.

Karp, Richard M.: See Gale (1970)

Kaupe 1962.
    Arthur F. Kaupe, Jr.
    Algorithm 144: treesort 1.
    CACM 5(1962)604.
    Modification of Floyd (1962).

Kautz 1959.
    William H. Kautz.
    Problem 59-8: A sorting problem.
    SIAM Rev. 1(1959)173.
    Conjectures that $[\log2(n!)]$ is a least upper bound (as well
        as a lower bound) on the number of comparisons required
        to sort n items.

Klammer 0000.
    W. Klammer.
    Sorting on a multiple magnetic tape unit.
    Electrodata Corp., 4 pp.
    Cited by Teichrow (1963). Not available from Electrodata.

Klammer 1956.
    Wallace Klammer.
    Sorting on a multiple magnetic tape unit.
    Proc. ACM Meeting 1956, p. 28.
    Cited by Youden (1965). Not found in interlibrary search.

Kloucek, J.: See Vlcek (1960)

Kloucek 1960.
    J. Kloucek and J. Vlcek.
    Navrh formulacni symbolicke soustavy pro ulohy z oblasti
        zpracovani hromadnych ekonomickych dat (Proposal for
        the symbolic formulation of a system for a portion of
        the domain of processing voluminous economic data).
    Symposium "Information Processing Machines" No. 8, Prague
        1960.
    Cited by Svoboda (1963).

Internal Sorting
84. Bibliography.

Knuth 1963.
     Donald L. Knuth.
     Length of strings for a merge sort.
     CACM 6(1963)685-8.
     Reviewed by Parker (1964).

Knuth 1963b.
     Donald E. Knuth.
     Letters to Editor.
     CACM 6(1963)585-7.
     Two letters on polyphase and cascade merges.

Kreuzer 1961.
     K. Kreuzer.
     Sortieren mit datenverarbeitenden Anlagen (Sorting with data
         processing machines).
     Elektron. Rechenanlagen 3,1(1961)7-13.
     Cited by de Beauclair (1961).

Kronmal, R.: See Cheydleur (1965), Tarter (1966)

Kronmal 1965.
     R.A. Kronmal and M.E. Tarter.
     Cumulative polygon address calculation sorting.
     Proc. ACM 20th National Conference, Cleveland, August 1965,
         pp. 376-85.
     Two improvements are described: 1) use of a polygon instead
         of a straight line for address calculation, 2) use of
         the original file space as part of the sorting space.
         (1) may require a preliminary counting pass over the
         file. (2) depends on reversing the sign of the items at
         the beginning and marking empty locations as 0; as each
         item is moved to its address-indicated place it is made
         positive to so indicate; if it displaces a negative
         item, then this item is next considered.

Landauer 1962.
     Walter I. Landauer.
     The tree as a strategem for automatic information handling.
     U. of Pennsylvania, PhD thesis, 1962. Moore School Report
         63-15. ASTIA AD293888.
     Cited by Lowe (1968).

Landauer 1962b.
     Walter I. Landauer and N.S. Prywes.
     A growing tree for descriptor translation.
     In "Symbolic Languages and Data Processing", Proceedings of
         a Symposium at Rome, Mar. 1962. Gordon and Breach, New
         York, 1962, pp. 153-172.
     Uses a balanced multibranched tree for keeping terms in sort
         as they are added.

Internal Sorting
84. Bibliography.

Landauer 1963.
    Walter I. Landauer.
    The balanced tree and its use in information retrieval.
    IEEE Trans. Electronic Computers, EC 12(1963)863.

Landis, E.M.: See Adel'son-Vel'skiy (1962)

Lautz 1963.
    W. Lautz.
    Sortierverfahren fur technische Dual-Computer (Sorting
        methods for a scientific binary computer).
    Elektron. Daten. 2(Apr 1963)69-81, 3(May 1963)133-41.
    Reviewed by Grisoff (1963). This two-part paper considers
        upward radix sorting (both decimal and binary) and
        merging, using magnetic tapes.

Lazarus, R.B.: See Frank (1960)

Lee, Tsai-Hwa: See McCracken (1959)

Lehmer 1957.
    D.H. Lehmer.
    Sorting cards with respect to a modulus.
    JACM 4(1957)41-46.
    Given an integer $m>1$, the problem is to separate the initial
        deck into m subdecks so that the contents of a given
        field, within each deck, are congruent mod m.

Lilly 1957.
    J.O. Lilly.
    Memory sort routine.
    SHARE NO SORT, 1 Feb 1957.
    Cited by Clapp (1959).

Lively 1960.
    J.A. Lively.
    Letter: remarks on amphisbaenic sorting.
    JACM 7(1960)187.
    This method (Nagler 1959) is not suitable for a general
        purpose sort.

Lombardi 1962.
    Lionello Lombardi.
    Mathematical structure of nonarithmetic data processing
        procedures.
    JACM 9(1962)136-59.
    A non-procedural language operating on files is described.

Internal Sorting
84. Bibliography.

London 1970.
      Ralph L. London.
      Certification of algorithm 245: Treesort 3.
      CACM 13(1970)371-3.
      This certification is by proof rather than by test. See
            criticism by Reddish (1971) and reply by London (1971).

London 1971.
      Ralph L. London.
      Reply to Reddish.
      CACM 14(1971)51.
      Reply to Reddish (1971) criticism of London (1970).

Lowe 1967.
      Thomas C. Lowe.
      Direct access memory retrieval using truncated record names.
      Software Age (Sep 1967)28-33.

Lowe 1968.
      Thomas C. Lowe.
      Encoding from alphanumeric names to record addresses.
      Software Age (Apr 1968)14-5, 28-32, 38.
      A review of methods.

Lozinskii, L.S.: See Pogrebinskii (1965)

Lozinskii 1965.
      L.S. Lozinskii.
      Internal sorting of information with a limited memory.
      Cybernetics 1,3(May-June 1965)60-4; English translation of
            Kibernetika 1,3(1965)58-62.
      Compares internal sorting methods, including a merge-in-
            place using a few extra cells to minimize shifting of
            the lower string being merged.

Lynch 1965.
      W.C. Lynch.
      More combinatorial properties of certain trees.
      CJ 7(1965)299-302.
      A recurrence relation is found for the probability that
            exactly i comparisons are needed to add the j-th item
            to a binary search tree, and the moments of the resul-
            ting distribution are determined.

Lytton 1956.
      J.G. Lytton and H.J. Holzman.
      Word insertion.
      SHARE RL0080, 20 Jun 1956.
      Cited by Clapp (1959).

Mackinney 1961.
     John G. Mackinney.
     Letter.
     JACM 8(1961)118.
     Comments on Nagler (1959).

MacLaren 1966.
     M. Donald MacLaren.
     Internal sorting by radix plus sifting.
     JACM 13(1966)404-11.
     A radix sort is made on the first p digits, and a final
          sifting pass completes the sort. Reviewed by Fox
          (1966).

MacLaughlin 1963.
     Dean S. MacLaughlin.
     A method of maintaining optimality in binary search trees.
     Computation Laboratory, Harvard University, Scientific
          Report No. ISR-4, 1 August 1963, Section II, 21 pages.
     Gives a procedure for maintaining near-equality of path
          lengths as items are added to the tree.

Malcolm 1963.
     W.D. Malcolm, Jr.
     String distribution for the polyphase sort.
     CACM 6(1963)217-20.

Mallows 1962.
     C.L. Mallows.
     Problem 62-2: Patience sorting.
     SIAM Rev. 2(1962)148-9.
     Sorting by dealing in a special way. Solution by proposer,
          SIAM Rev. 5(1963)375-6.

Manker 1963.
     Harold H. Manker.
     Multiphase sorting.
     CACM 6(1963)214-7.
     A polyphase system for four tapes.

Mankin, Efrem S.: See Brawn (1969), Brawn (1970)

Internal Sorting
84. Bibliography.

Mauchly 1948.
    John W. Mauchly.
    Sorting and collating.
    Lecture delivered 25 July 1946. Published in vol. III of
        "Theory and Techniques for Design of Electronic Digital
        Computers", University of Pennsylvania, Moore School of
        Electrical Engineering, Report No. 48-9, 30 June 1948,
        as Lecture 22, 20 pp.
    Describes 'digital sorting' (upward and downward radix
        sorts); ranking and binary ranking sorts; 'collation'
        (merging); 'classification' (downward variable radix
        sort). Applications to external sorting are discussed.

McAllester 1964.
    R.L. McAllester.
    Polyphase sorting with overlapped rewind.
    CACM 7(1964)158-9.

McCool 1956a.
    T.C. McCool.
    704 Block sort program.
    SHARE NSSRT-1, 14 Sep 1956.
    Cited by Clapp (1959).

McCool 1956b.
    T.C. McCool.
    704 Merge program.
    SHARE NSMRG-1.
    Cited by Clapp (1959).

McCracken 1959.
    Daniel D. McCracken, Harold Weiss and Tsai-Hwa Lee.
    Programming Business Computers.
    John Wiley and Sons, New York, 1959. xvii+510 pp.
    Chapter 15 deals specifically with sorting.

McCreight,E.: See Bayer (1970)

McKellar, A.C.: See Frazer (1969), Frazer (1970)

Mendoza 1962.
    A.G. Mendoza.
    A dispersion pass algorithm for the polyphase merge.
    CACM 5(1962)502-4.
    Reviewed by Carter (1963).

Internal Sorting
84. Bibliography.

Moeller 1961.
     D. Moeller.
     MR 1401 - A generalized sort program for the Card-RAMAC
          1401.
     IBM Systems Engineering Conference, New York, 1961.
     Cited by Carter (1962). Not found in interlibrary search.

Morris 1969.
     Robert Morris.
     Some theorems on sorting.
     SIAM J. Appl. Math. 17(1969)1-6.
     Shows that the lower bound on the number of comparisons
          required for a sort is $\log2(n!)$ or greater.

Nagler 1959.
     H. Nagler.
     Amphisbaenic sorting.
     JACM 6(1959)459-68.
     If p+1 tapes are available, this method does a radix sort to
          base p, using tapes as bins, most significant digit
          first. Discussion: Lively (1960), Nagler (1961),
          Mackinney (1961).

Nagler 1960.
     H. Nagler.
     An estimation of the relative efficiency of two internal
          sorting methods.
     CACM 3(1960)618-20.
     Compares two internal sorts on IBM 705: two-way merge and
          binary search. Reviewed by Grau (1961).

Nagler 1961.
     H. Nagler.
     Letter.
     JACM 8(1961)117.
     Reply to Lively (1960).

NCR 1962a.
     National Cash Register Company.
     NCR 315: sort generator magnetic tape.
     Sept 1962.
     Cited by Teichrow (1963).

NCR 1962b.
     National Cash Register Company.
     NCR 315: sort generator CRAM.
     Dec 1962.
     Cited by Teichrow (1963).

Nelson, R.J.: See Bose (1961), Bose (1962)

Internal Sorting
84. Bibliography.

Nichols 1962.
    J.H. Nichols and A. Tiedrich.
    A multi-variant generalized sort program employing auxiliary
        drum storage.
    Proc. ACM Meeting 1962, 102-3.
    Describes a sort generator which keeps keys in core and the
        rest of the record on a drum.

Nivat 1965.
    Nivat.
    Permutations et tris (Permutations and sorts).
    Institut de Programmation, Paris, 1965.
    Cited by Picard (1966).

Oettinger 1957.
    Anthony G. Oettinger.
    Account identification for automatic data processing.
    JACM 4(1957)245-53.
    Uses Huffman minimal redundancy codes for keys, to reduce
        the time required for downward radix sorting.

Outrata 1966.
    Edvard Outrata.
    A special sorting algorithm.
    Stroje na Zpracovani Informaci (Information Processing
        Machines) 12(1966)275-81.
    A sequence of integers is "sorted" on a decimal machine by
        packing two tenary digits per decimal digit, assigning
        these ternary digits (in order) to the n possible
        integers of the sequence, and initializing to zeroes.
        The first time a number is met in the input, set its
        digit to 1; the next time it is met set its digit to 2;
        thereafter leave its digit unchanged.

Park, T.M.: See Smart (1960)

Parker 1964.
    E.T. Parker.
    Review of Knuth (1963).
    CR 5(1964)173 #5748.

Paterson 1963.
    J.B. Paterson.
    The COBOL sort verb.
    CACM 6(1963)255-8.
    Describes manner of use, relation to standard sort packages.

Internal Sorting
84. Bibliography.

Patt 1969.
    Yale N. Patt.
    Variable length tree structures having minimum average
        search time.
    CACM 12(1969)72-6.

Peterson 1955.
    W.W. Peterson.
    Sorting on data processing systems.
    Lecture at the University of Michigan Special Summer Con-
        ference on Digital Computers and Data Procesors, August
        1955. Published in the Proceedings of that same con-
        ference in 1956.
    Upward radix and merging sorts are discussed.

Peterson 1957.
    W.W. Peterson.
    Addressing for random-access storage.
    IBM Journal 1(1957) 130-46.
    This paper, usually cited as the first source for the hash
        coding technique, acknowledges its invention in 1954 by
        Samuel, Amdahl and Boehme. Much of the discussion is
        relevant to address sorting.

Peto 1970.
    Richard Peto.
    Remark on algorithm 347.
    CACM 13(1970)624.
    An improvement in Singleton (1969).

Philco 1961.
    Philco Corporation.
    Electronic data processing systems: Philco 2000 sort genera-
        tor.
    TM 17, Nov 1961.
    Cited by Teichrow (1963).

Picard 1962.
    Claude Picard.
    Cheminement optimum et theorie de l'information.
    IFIP Congress, 1962, p. 720.
    Cited by Picard (1966).

Picard 1965.
    Claude Picard.
    Toward optimal sorting strategies.
    Proc. IFIP Congress 1965. Spartan Books, Washington, and
        Macmillan, London. 1966. vol. II pp. 461-3.
    A brief and theoretical treatment of binary insertion sort-
        ing.

Internal Sorting
84. Bibliography.

Picard 1965b.
    Claude Picard.
    Problemes de traitment de l'information et questionnaires.
    4th Congres de traitment de l'information (AFIRO, Versailles, 1964) Dunod, Paris, 1965.
    Cited by Picard (1966).

Picard 1965c.
    Claude Picard.
    Theorie des questionnaires.
    Gauthiers-Villars, Paris, 1965.
    Cited by Picard (1966).

Picard 1966.
    Claude Picard.
    Quelques idees recentes sur le probleme du tri (Some recent ideas on the sorting problem).
    Revue Francais de Traitment de l'Informatique: CHIFFRES 9,1(1966)41-6.
    Reviewed by Grandage (1966). Discusses "questionnaires", or decision trees. Gives an Algol procedure for a binary ranking sort (par. 45), except that instead of looking at the midpoint of each segment he looks nearer one end or the other depending on a priori knowledge of existing bias.

Pogrebinskii 1965.
    S.B. Pogrebinskii and L.S. Lozinskii.
    On the problem of sorting information by means of magnetic tapes.
    Cybernetics 1,2(Mar-Apr 1965)74-80; English translation from Kibernetika 1,2(1965)73-79.
    Compares an N by N split merge with binary radix sort, least significant bit first.

Pratt, R.D.: See Johnson (1958)

Prywes, N.S.: See Landauer (1962)

Prywes 1962.
    N.S. Prywes and H.J. Gray.
    The multi-list system for real-time storage and retrieval.
    IFIP Congress, 1962, p. 273.
    Cited by Picard (1966).

Rabinovitch, Z.L.: See Gladun (1965)

Internal Sorting
84. Bibliography.

Radke 1966.
      C.E. Radke.
      Merge-sort analysis by matrix techniques.
      IBM Systems J. 5(1966)226-47.
      Carter (1962) used difference equations to analyze unbalan-
          ced merging methods. The present paper represents the
          difference equations by matrices and gets various
          properties of the merges by matrix multiplication.

Randell 1962.
      B. Randell.
      Remark on algorithm 76: sorting procedures.
      CACM 5(1962)348.
      Corrections to Flores (1962).

Randell 1963.
      B. Randell and L.J. Russell.
      Certification of algorithms 63, 64, and 65: Partition,
          Quicksort, Find.
      CACM 6(1963)446.
      See Hoare (1961).

Ranshaw 1961.
      Russell W. Ranshaw.
      Certification of algorithm 23: mathsort.
      CACM 4(1961)238.
      See Feurzeig (1960).

RCA 1961.
      Radio Corporation of America.
      Design specifications for ASCI-MATIC Sort and Merge System.
      Astro-Electronics Div. of RCA and Applied Data Research,
          Inc. Report SR-61-3, June 1961. Prepared for Off. Asst.
          Chief of Staff for Intelligence, Dept. Army.
      Cited by Teichrow (1963).

Rechard 1961.
      Ottis W. Rechard.
      Review of Flores (1960).
      CR 2(1960) 36 #602.

Reddish, K.A.: See Griffin (1970)

Reddish 1971.
      K.A. Reddish.
      Comment on London's certification of Algorithm 245.
      CACM 14(1971)50-1.
      Criticizes London (1970) on the ground that proof of an
          algorithm does not prove that the code is correct.

Internal Sorting
84. Bibliography.

Reynolds 1961.
    S.W. Reynolds.
    A generalized polyphase merge algorithm.
    CACM 4(1961)347-9. Addendum p. 495.
    A procedure for tape merging.

Rhodes 1955.
    Ida Rhodes and Mary Elizabeth Stevens.
    Preliminary report on a combined sorting-file merging method
        for electronic data processing.
    NBS Report 3155, Mar. 1955.
    No discussion of internal sorting.

Rodriguez 1963.
    Fernando L.T. Rodriguez.
    Review of Carter (1962).
    CR 4(1963)33 #3594.

Russell, L.J.: See Randell (1963)

Sander-Cederlof 1970.
    Robert B. Sander-Cederlof.
    Supersort: high speed sort subroutine for the Control Data
        3300.
    Proceedings of Focus-3 Conference, St. Paul, 25-27 May 1970.
        Control Data Company, Palo Alto, Calif., pp. 251-72.
    Supersort is a version of Quicksort using the median of
        three items as partition bound and using the ranking
        sort for segments of 11 items or less. Timing com-
        parison with minima, bubble, and ranking sorts on
        timeshared 3300. Fortran and Compass versions of pro-
        gram are given.

Sandier, G.: See Darnaut (1962)

Savastano, Sal, Jr.: See Falkin (1963)

Savidge 1955.
    D.V. Savidge.
    Arranger: ten word item 10x10.
    Remington Rand, Oct 1955.
    Describes a routine for Univac tape sort of ten-word items
        on up to ten keys. Replacement-selection used to form
        initial strings. Provision is made for operator control
        of merge passes.

Internal Sorting
84. Bibliography.

Schensted 1961.
    C.E. Schensted.
    Longest increasing and decreasing sequences.
    Canad. J. Math 13(1961)179-91.
    The number of sequences of length 'n which have longest
        monotone subsequences of length m is investigated by
        means of Young tableaux.

Schick 1963.
    Thomas Schick.
    Disk file sorting.
    CACM 6(1963)330-1, 339.
    Key versus record sorting on IBM 1401 with disk. Reviewed by
        Hendrix (1963).

Schubert 1963.
    George R. Schubert.
    Certification of algorithm 175: shuttle sort.
    CACM 6(1962)619.
    See Shaw (1963).

Schwartz 0000.
    B.L. Schwartz.
    Mathematical analysis of sorting procedures.
    WADC Tech. Rep. 53-505, appendix B.
    Cited by Hosken (1955).

Schwartz 1955.
    B.L. Schwartz.
    Criteria for comparing methods of sorting.
    Paper at ACM Conf., Sept 1955. Battelle Memorial Institute
        Report.
    Cited by Teichrow (1963). Not found in interlibrary search.

Scidmore 1963.
    A.K. Scidmore and B.L. Weinberg.
    Storage and search properties of a tree-organized memory
        system.
    CACM 6(1963)28-31.

Scowen 1965.
    R.S. Scowen.
    Algorithm 271: Quickersort.
    CACM 8(1965)669-70.
    Version of Quicksort using center element as median estim-
        ate. Certified by Blair (1966).

Internal Sorting
84. Bibliography.

Scowen 1969.
    R.S. Scowen.
    Notes on algorithms 25 and 26.
    CJ 12(1969)408-9.
    Points out that these algorithms (Boothroyd 1967) slow down
        when several items are equal. Corrects error for a file
        with a single item.

Sedlacek, S.: See Vlcek (1960)

Seward 1954.
    Harold H. Seward.
    Information sorting in the application of electronic digital
        computers to business application.
    ASTIA 35462. MIT Digital Computer Lab. Report R-232, Mas-
        ter's Thesis, 1954.
    Cited by Teichrow (1963).

Shapin 1954.
    Ted Shapin.
    Illiac Library Subroutine W2(134).
    Univ. Illinois, 1954.
    Cited by Douglas 1959 as a ranking sort.

SHARE 1958.
    Three-way sort-merge program.
    SHARE NSSRT-2, NSMRG-2, 21 Jan 1958.
    Cited by Clapp (1959).

SHARE 1959.
    General data files and processing.
    SHARE Comm. on Theory of Inform. Handling Report TIH-1,
        SSD-71, Item C-1663, 22 pp.
    Cited by Teichrow (1963).

SHARE 1961.
    Preparation of sorted reports.
    9PAC User's Reference Manual, IBM corrected through Aug.
        1961, pp. 143-6.
    Cited by Teichrow (1963).

Shaw 1959.
    C.J. Shaw.
    The organization, retrieval and sorting of information in a
        digital computer.
    Systems Development Corp. FN-1384, S-1. May 1959.
    Cited by Teichrow (1963).

Internal Sorting
84. Bibliography.

Shaw 1963.
     C.J. Shaw and T.N. Trimble.
     Algorithm 175: shuttle sort.
     CACM 6(1963) 312-3.
     Exchanges adjacent pairs. Certified by Schubert (1963),
          criticized by Juelich (1963).

Shell 1959.
     D.L. Shell.
     A high-speed sorting procedure.
     CACM 2,7(Jul 1959) 30-2.
     Describes the "Shell Sort" procedure for internal sorting in
          place, with flowchart, 704 program, and sample times
          for 500 to 20,000 items.

Sherwood, F.: See Feerst (1959)

Shiowitz 1954.
     Marc Shiowitz.
     Digital computer programs for data sorting problems.
     National Cash Register Co., Hawthorne, Calif.; Lecture notes
          for summer session at Wayne Univ., 1954.
     Cited by Hosken (1955).

Singleton, R.C.: See Isaac (1956)

Singleton 1969.
     Richard C. Singleton.
     Algorithm A347: An efficient algorithm for sorting with
          minimal storage.
     CACM 12(1969) 185-7.
     Version of Quicksort with median estimated from a sample of
          three items, final segments of length 11 or less sorted
          by bubble sort. FORTRAN and ALGOL versions given. See
          Griffin (1970), Peto (1970).

Smart 1960.
     R.G. Smart and T.M. Park.
     Frequency distribution sorting on UTECOM.
     Australian National Committee on Computation and Automatic
          Control: Automatic Computing in Australia, Sydney, May
          1960, A6.3.
     Cited by Youden (1965). Not found in interlibrary search.

Sobel 1962.
     Sheldon Sobel.
     Oscillating sort - a new merge sorting technique.
     JACM 9(1962) 372-4.
     This procedure gives an (n-1) way merge with n tapes.

Internal Sorting
84. Bibliography.

Soden 0000.
    Walter Soden.
    Sorting numbers into sequence on a digital computer.
    Computer Control Co., Point Mugu.
    Cited by Hosken (1955). Not available from CCC.

Stevens, M.E.: See Rhodes (1955)

Stringer 1960.
    I.B. Stringer.
    Sorting techniques for automatic computers.
    Post Office El. Engrs. Journ. 53,3(Oct 1960)181-3.
    Cited by de Beauclair (1961).

Sussenguth 0000.
    E.H. Sussenguth, Jr.
    A study of procedures for frequency counting of words in
        running text.
    Harvard Computation Lab. Report ISR-4.
    Cited by Teichrow (1963).

Sussenguth 1963.
    Edward H. Sussenguth, Jr.
    Use of tree structures for processing files.
    CACM 6(1963)272-9.
    An average filial set size of 3.6 is optimum for a tree to
        be searched.

Svoboda 1963.
    Jan Svoboda.
    Sorting by repeated comparison with alternating directions
        of comparison.
    Stroje na Zpracovani Informaci (Information Processing
        Machines) 9(1963)141-149.
    Reviewed by Gear (1966). Shows that alternating transposi-
        tion (par. 39) is about 25% shorter than transposition
        (par. 38) on the National Elliot 803b computer.

Tani 1956.
    P. Tani.
    Sorting subroutine-minimum space.
    SHARE NA-020, 26 Mar 1956.
    Cited by Clapp (1959).

Tarter, M.: See Cheydleur (1965), Kronmal (1965)

Internal Sorting
84. Bibliography.

Tarter 1966.
        Michael E. Tarter and Richard A. Kronmal.
        Non-uniform key distribution and address calculation sort-
                ing.
        Proc. 21st Nat. Conf. ACM. Thompson Book Co., Washington,
                1966, pp. 331-7.
        Uses cumulative polygon address function to compensate for
                non-uniform distribution of keys.

Teichrow 1963.
        D. Teichrow.
        Bibliography: sorting.
        CACM 6(1963)280.
        This bibliography was prepared to accompany the papers from
                the ACM Sort Symposium, Nov 1962, Princeton.

Thuring 1957.
        B. Thuring.
        Die Logik der Programmierung.
        Teil I of 'Methoden der Programmierung', Robert Goeller
                Verlag, Baden-Baden, 1957, page 217ff.
        Cited by Boehm (1961a) for the counting sort.

Tiedrich, A.: See Nichols (1962)

Toth, Gloria S.: See Goetz (1963b)

Trimble, T.N.: See Shaw (1963)

TRW 1963.
        Thompson Ramo Wooldridge, Inc.
        TRW-530 generalized sort program (Sort I). Preliminary
                writeup.
        25 Jan 1963.
        Cited by Teichrow (1963). Not available from TRW.

Univac 1952.
        Eckert-Mauchly Division of Remington Rand, Inc.
        965-1, Sep 1952.
        Cited by Hosken (1955).

Univac 1954.
        Univac Division of Sperry Rand Corporation.
        Sorting methods for Univac system.
        1954.
        Cited by Hosken (1955).

Internal Sorting
84. Bibliography.

Univac 1955.
    Univac Division of Sperry Rand Corporation.
    Catalog of Univac system routines.
    1955.
    Cited by Hosken (1955).

van der Poel 1964.
    W.L. van der Poel.
    Review of Hibbard (1963b).
    CR 5(1964)27 #5032.

Vanek,V.: See Vlcek (1960)

van Emden 1970.
    M.H. van Emden.
    Increasing the efficiency of Quicksort.
    CACM 13(1970)563-7.
    The use of a bounding interval instead of an assumed median
        improved sorting time by about 15% over Hoare's Quick-
        sort. See par. 57.

van Emden 1970b.
    M.H. van Emden.
    Algorithm 402: Increasing the efficiency of Quicksort.
    CACM 13(1970)693-4.
    This is the Algol procedure described in van Emden (1970).

van Lint 1960.
    J.H. van Lint.
    Problem 60-8: Another sorting problem.
    SIAM Rev. 2(1960)217.
    Concerns maximum monotone subsequences. Solution by proposer
        SIAM Rev. 3(1961)336-7.

Venn 1958.
    J.L. Venn.
    Letter.
    CJ 1(1958)123.
    The argument in Bell (1958) for 2 as the base of selection
        is invalid.

Vlcek, J.: See Kloucek (1960)

Internal Sorting
84. Bibliography.

Vlcek 1960.
    J. Vlcek, S. Sedlacek, V. Vanek and J. Kloucek.
    Zaklady methodiky programovani automatickeho zpracovani
        hromadnych ekonomickych dat (Principles of a program-
        ming method for automatic processing of voluminous
        economic data).
    Final report of the Research Institute of Mathematical
        Machines, Prague, 1960.
    Cited by Svoboda (1963).

von Neumann, John: See Goldstine (1948)

Waks 1963.
    David J. Waks.
    Conversion, reconversion and comparison techniques in
        variable-length sorting.
    CACM 6(1963)267-72.

Weinberg, B.L.: See Scidmore (1963)

Weiss, Harold: See McCracken (1959)

Weissblum 1960.
    Walter Weissblum.
    Problem 60-12: A sorting problem.
    SIAM Rev. 2(1960)298.
    Average length of maximal contiguous monotonic subsequences
        is 2.4203. Solution by proposer: SIAM Rev. 9(1967)121-
        2.

Wierzbowski 1965.
    Jan Wierzbowski.
    Sorting by means of random access store.
    Polska Akademia Nauk, Instytut Masyn Matematycznych, Algory-
        tmy 2,4(1965)59-68.
    Sorting by insertion in a doubly-linked list, with or
        without a separate directory of segments to avoid a
        complete scan from the head of the list.

Williams 1964.
    J.W.J. Williams.
    Algorithm 232: heapsort.
    CACM 7(1964)347-8.

Windley 1959.
    P.F. Windley.
    The influence of storage access time on merging processes in
        a computer.
    CJ 2(1959)49-50.
    Reviewed by Gotleib (1961). Gives formulas and tables for
        choice of order of tape merge, blocking factor, etc.

Internal Sorting
84. Bibliography.

Windley 1960.
        P.F. Windley.
        Trees, forests and rearranging.
        CJ 3(1960) 84-88.
        A sorting method which puts each item in turn into a binary
            tree is described and analyzed. The number of com-
            parisons required is the same as for Quicksort (Hoare
            1962), but 3N additional locations are required for
            pointers.

Woodall 1969.
        A.D. Woodall.
        Algorithm 43: a listed radix sort.
        CJ 12(1969) 406.
        Algol procedure for increasing radix sort using simple list
            surrogate.

Woodall 1970.
        A.D. Woodall.
        Algorithm 45: an internal sorting procedure using a two-way
            merge.
        CJ 13(1970) 110-1.
        This Algol procedure forms initial strings as long as pos-
            sible, working in the direction established by the
            first two items in each new string. Simple list surro-
            gate is used.

Woodrum 1969.
        L.J. Woodrum.
        Internal sorting with minimal comparing.
        IBM Systems J. 8(1969) 189-203.
        The internal sort used in APL is a two way merge using a
            single pointer vector. Expected number of comparisons
            is derived and tabulated. Algorithm given in APL.

Wyatt 1957.
        J.B. Wyatt.
        Logical memory sort-minimum time.
        SHARE CF058, 26 Dec 1957.
        Cited by Clapp (1959).

Wyatt 1958a.
        J.B. Wyatt.
        Generalized tape sorting routine.
        SHARE CF064, 14 Apr 1958.
        Cited by Clapp (1959).

Internal Sorting
84. Bibliography.

Wyatt 1958b.
      J.B. Wyatt.
      Generalized memory sorting routine.
      SHARE CF065, 5 May 1958.
      Cited by Clapp (1959).

Yarbrough 1969.
      L.D. Yarbrough.
      Review of Flores (1969).
      CR 10(1969)49 #16053.

Yates, Thomas L.: See Flies (1969)

Youden 1965.
      W.W. Youden.
      Computer literature bibliography 1946 to 1963.
      NBS Misc. Pub. 266, 31 Mar 1965, 463 pp.

Yucel 1970.
      M. Nadir Yucel.
      Note on radix sort.
      IEEE Transactions C-19(1970)653.
      Computes information-theoretic change due to radix sorting.

Yuval 1967.
      G. Yuval.
      A new sorting scheme and its applications (Hebrew).
      Proc. 2nd National (Israeli) Conf. on Data Processing, p.
            321-3.
      Reviewed by Harel (1967).

Zorberbier 1960.
      Werner Zorberbier.
      Vergleichende Betrachtungen zum Magnetbandsortieren (Com-
            parative considerations in magnetic tape sorting).
      Elektronische Datenverarbeitung 5(1960)28-44.
      Gives discussion, formulas and curves for various tape
            sorting procedures.